The Peter Plan
A Proposal for Survival

Books by Laurence J. Peter

The Peter Plan
Individual Instruction
Classroom Instruction
Therapeutic Instruction
Teacher Education
The Peter Prescription
The Peter Principle (with Raymond Hull)
Prescriptive Teaching

The Peter Plan
A Proposal for Survival

by
Laurence J. Peter

Illustrated by Walter Griba

William Morrow and Company, Inc.
NEW YORK • 1976

Lines by Robinson Jeffers on page 11
by courtesy of Random House, Inc.

Printed in the United States of America.

2   3   4   5   79   78   77   76   75

Library of Congress Cataloging in Publication Data

Peter, Laurence J
    The Peter plan.

    Includes index.
      1. Human ecology—United States. 2. Environmental policy—United States. 3. Progress.
    I. Title.
GF503.P47   301.31′0973   75-22327
ISBN 0-688-02972-8

BOOK DESIGN: H. ROBERTS

To all those who, while trying to be part
of the solution, recognize that they are
still part of the problem

CONTENTS

Preamble

There comes a time in the affairs of men when you
must take the bull by the tail and face the situation.
—W. C. FIELDS

WE worry about the future with unprecedented fervor. We
know our lakes are dying, our rivers are growing dirtier, our
atmosphere is becoming increasingly polluted, and we live
under the brooding threat of a nuclear holocaust. We are
aware that oppressive poverty exists in the midst of affluence.
We see our once-great cities deteriorating. We are threatened
as members of the human species because we understand that
the problems of warfare, population, and environment do not
stop at our national borders. The planet is facing disaster.
Our concern is well justified. It is time to do something about
the problem. If we are not too late, it is within reason that we
can be successful.

The pace of events is so fast that unless we can
find some way to keep our sights on tomorrow, we
cannot expect to be in touch with today.*
—DEAN RUSK

During the period in which these problems were developing
we were satisfied that advancing technology and escalation of

---

* Throughout this book I have inserted quotes so that you can see what
others have to say regarding the topics under discussion.

9

the gross national product would solve our problems and bring us to the fulfillment of a world of peace and prosperity. If we could not be certain of God's intentions, we could always be certain of Science.

> We were in greater peril in the complacent years, when all of the present evils were in existence or brewing but were layered over by our national smugness.
>
> —JOHN GARDNER

We would all like to find simple solutions to the complexities of the threats to human survival. Seeking such simplicity, ardent but irrational minds fall prey to mysticism, and to every nostrum or panacea that promises an easy solution.

> Humankind cannot bear very much reality.
>
> —T. S. ELIOT

On November 3, 1973, the United States launched Mariner 10. It traveled to Venus and then orbited Mercury. It performed magnificently and sent back pictures taken during its billion-mile flight. Mariner 10 took years of planning. But social planning—and foreseeing energy and food shortages before they happen—have not been functions of government and are regarded by some as slightly sinister.

> A government that robs Peter to pay Paul can always depend upon the support of Paul.
>
> —G. B. SHAW

Most of us are greatly skilled at self-exoneration and enormously talented at shifting blame to others. Granted, responsibility is widely distributed. There are dishonest persons who perpetrate corruption for profit throughout every level of society. There are those who cheat and lie to consumers and engage in all manner of questionable practices. There are extremists of the Right and of the Left who behave as though hatred and violence will pave the way to a better future.

There are those of power and influence who could effect constructive change of our institutions, but who protect their vested interests and disregard humanity's future. There are the majority of citizens who are complacent about the impending crisis so long as they are supplied with essential consumer goods and some luxuries. Apathy can be even more harmful than antipathy to the human condition. They are loathe to risk discomfort for the common good of mankind. They are more disposed to risk mankind.

> Life is like a sewer—you get out of it what you
> put into it.
>
> —TOM LEHRER

In spite of widespread selfishness and complacency there are hopeful signs we are entering a new period of awareness, characterized by a deeper respect for the natural world. This includes a recognition that our fate as individuals is inseparable from our fate as a species and the future of other forms of life that make their home on this planet.

> . . . the greatest beauty
> is organic wholeness,
>   the wholeness
> of life and things,
> the divine beauty
> of the universe
>   Love that,
> not man apart from that . . .
>
> —ROBINSON JEFFERS

This book presents what is hoped to be a commonsense approach to the survival of mankind, along with insistence on the maintenance of the best of his achievements. This seems to be asking a lot. But we must ask the most or we may end with nothing.

The Peter Plan completes a trilogy that began with *The Peter Principle,* an explanation of how individuals escalate to their respective levels of incompetence. A second volume, *The Peter Prescription,* demonstrated how individuals could avoid their levels of incompetence. This final volume, *The Peter Plan,* shows ways by which we can protect our planet while civilization moves confidently forward to new achievements to secure the future for the human race. This book is presented in three parts:

The Peter Proliferation shows you where we are today and how tomorrow could be doomsday or a new day.

The Peter Planet provides you with a vision of what the world could be like if we could use even a fraction of our moral, mental, and technological capabilities to assure our survival in a state of well-being.

The Peter Program presents practical strategies to bring about the kind of world needed to fulfill man's optimum potential in a society capable of continuous renewal.

> In all things that are purely social we can be as separate as the fingers, yet one as the hand in all things essential to mutual progress.
> —BOOKER T. WASHINGTON

PART ONE

The Peter Proliferation

Carriages without horses shall go,
And accidents fill the world with woe
Around the world thoughts shall fly
In the twinkling of an eye.
                    —M. (MOTHER) SHIPTON
                        1488–1561 A.D.

CHAPTER I

Peril

Towards what ultimate point is society tending by
its industrial progress? When the progress ceases,
in what condition are we to expect that it will leave
mankind?
—JOHN STUART MILL, 1857

I WAS born in Excelsior City* over a half-century ago. My
forefathers were pioneer farmers. I am a member of the first
generation to grow up in the suburbs of the city. I have been
witness to the city's growth from its beginnings as a seaport
and supply center for farms, logging companies, and mining
operations to its present position as an industrial, commercial,
residential megalopolis that dominates the county and the life-
style of its people.

* Author's Note: I was born and grew up in Vancouver, B. C., Canada.
Many of the observations leading to the discovery of the Peter Principle
were made while working for the public school systems in and around that
city. In writing this trilogy—*The Peter Princple, The Peter Prescription,*
and *The Peter Plan*—Excelsior City was created as the mythical setting for
the cases presented because the word "excelsior" means always upward. I
have continued to investigate incompetence during my residence in several
American cities. If you were to ask me why I have persisted in my pursuit of
incompetence, I could only give you Sir George Mallory's instinctive reply,
"Because it is there." I presently live in Los Angeles, California, so that
Excelsior City now encompasses much more than my birthplace.

His great ambition was to escape civilization, and as
soon as he had money he went to Southern California.
—ALVA JOHNSTON

15

When I was a boy, little was expected of the city fathers. If the mayor and members of the council did nothing to embarrass the city or besmirch its good name, the residents were satisfied. This situation changed as the city grew and urbanization flourished. During the period of Excelsior City's rapid expansion the promise of the future lay in the hands of men like Jeremiah Beachslic, Rob R. Baron, and J. P. Getall. These leaders of industry and commerce were regarded as heroes. Their words describing never-ending expansion of markets, exploitation of resources, and promises of an ever-rising standard of living became the foundation of the American Dream.

Excelsior City had not set out to be a city-state.

Excelsior City had not set out to be a city-state; it was something that happened along the way. Only yesterday, it seems, my grandparents were out in tranquil Excelsior Valley, working the farm and living close to nature. Occasionally they would drive to the city to buy supplies, poke around in the stores, treat themselves to a ride on a trolley car, or watch a haircut. Now we are all packed into the city or jammed up on the freeway trying to get to work on time. There was nothing orderly about the way it came to pass. We lived through it, but leapt from being rural to being urban without conscious knowledge of the metamorphosis.

> City life: Millions of people being lonesome together.
> —HENRY DAVID THOREAU

Excelsior City expansion provided jobs, and this in turn provided a labor pool. Excelsior Mattress, Inc., Mercury Paper Mills, Irwin Blight Construction Co., and other companies did not build in the wilderness, but chose the city, where there was a dependable labor force, water, power, transportation, tax concessions, and a market for their products. The factories went to the city, workers proliferated, commerce escalated, and Excelsior City boomed.

The city is where the action is. The city is where you find the best stores, theaters, libraries, restaurants, art galleries, and cultural centers. These fine advantages more than offset the penalties the city extracts in violent crimes, crowding, pollution, bureaucratic hassles, and traffic jams. Also, welfare is easier to obtain and more rewarding in the city.

> All cities are mad: but the madness is gallant. All cities are beautiful: but the beauty is grim.
> —CHRISTOPHER MORLEY

Excelsior City continued to expand, despite the doomsayers' cries of TOO MUCH—TOO RAPID. Developers bought tracts of land and created new communities—Excelsior Heights, Excelsior Lake Park, and Excelsior Retirement Village. These pseudocommunities were scarcely more than mere housing projects and further isolated potentially influential citizens from any real involvement in, or awareness of the plight of the city. The poor were left to enjoy substandard housing, as the cost of new homes doubled in the city. *Payoffs* became the blot on the city's escutcheon, and increase of appetite grew by what it fed on. Greedy developers bulldozed new territory without regard for the area being defaced or its relationship to conservation, erosion, or the capacity of Excelsior City resources.

Developers obtained tracts of land and created new subdivisions.

Political leadership in Excelsior City reflected these developments and furthered them. Mayor R. Kive, member of one of the first families and patron of the arts, was voted out of office in favor of Pat C. Leeder, loyal friend and supporter of big business. He was followed by Hank E. Panky, who became quite wealthy during his three terms in office. Each year on his birthday he was given a $100-a-plate testimonial dinner attended by all the major contractors doing business with the city. The proceeds went into a tax-deductible trust fund administered by Panky's cousin, Kith N. Kin. Upon his retirement from politics, it was reported by the *Excelsior Daily*

Log that Hank E. Panky had received stock in Beachslic Oil at the time of the granting of offshore drilling rights in Excelsior Bay. Rob R. Baron, III, president of the Baron National Bank, had purchased a lifetime, all-expense-paid membership for Mayor Panky in the Excelsior County Club, an exclusive organization that excluded nearly everyone. City government had become a vessel that was sinking from leaks at the top.

> Today, if you are not confused
> you are just not thinking clearly.
> —IRENE PETER

When the knavery of the political-industrial complex became known to them, the latter-day residents of Excelsior City realized they had put the foxes in charge of the hen house, and they had been sold the cackle without the eggs. With eyes finally opened, they saw they were living in a decomposing environment, assailed by noxious daily doses of chemical fumes, sewage, smoke, noise, filth, and ugliness in the midst of urban and moral decay. In the unstable economy, prices skyrocketed. As a young, poorly paid teacher, I ended up in a high-rent district without even moving. Just when I saved enough money to buy something, I found it was no longer enough.

> Money is round. It rolls away.
> —SHOLOM ALEICHEM

The anguish of the poor and the racially oppressed turned increasingly to violence and crime. Rising taxes and prices, along with shortages of food, the energy crisis, and strikes interrupted essential services and resulted in disenchantment and a feeling of betrayal by contemporary city life and a longing for the good days of simple graft.

> A trust is known by the companies it keeps.
> —ELLIS O. JONES

The nostalgia craze of the early 1970s resulted in people's collecting memorabilia from an earlier, more stable period and

I ended up in a high-rent district without even moving.

electing C. Nyle as reform, law-and-order mayor. Nyle conducted an all-out war against the youth culture, subversives, dissidents, certain minorities, intellectuals, freedom of the press, and birth control. He championed the cause of individual responsibility in matters of charity and welfare. His motto was, "Least government—best government," quasi-quoting Thomas Jefferson, who he otherwise detested. C. Nyle extolled the virtues of patriotism, hard work, thrift, self-denial, family, church, motherhood, and minding your own business. At the same time, his depredations were such he could have been indicted for giving dirty politics a bad name. Meanwhile organized crime and malicious exploitation of the environment flourished.

> I needed the good will of the legislature of four
> states. I formed the legislative bodies with my own
> money. I found it cheaper that way.
>   —JAY GOULD

In the world beyond Excelsior City, the technologically developed nations were leading the underdeveloped countries on a parallel mission of destruction. Man and the nature he corrupted were speeding, arm in arm, toward extinction. The Peter Proliferation was ravaging the planet. Obsessive hunger for growth, escalation, and an ever-increasing GNP (gross national product) were pillaging man's heritage. The dream that economic growth was always an unmixed blessing had become our nightmare.

> When nations grow old
> the Arts grow cold,
> And commerce settles on
> every tree.
> —WILLIAM BLAKE

I began my preparation for a professional career in 1938 when I enrolled in my first course in teacher education. In my quest for answers to the problems of public education and the perils of mankind, I continued my formal education long after I became a practicing teacher. As a matter of fact, my devotion to the task was such that I enrolled in various professional courses each year for twenty-five consecutive years. This enduring pursuit of knowledge was initially motivated by a desire to improve my own teaching and later by a desire to improve the education of other teachers, thereby increasing their competence as teachers.

I began by studying the physical sciences and gradually was drawn to the social sciences. I found a strange disparity between the sciences of inert matter and those of life. It appeared that our scientific knowledge was outdistancing our faltering social progress. Science and technology had developed a world of their own based upon monumental calculations and abstractions, taking into account all factors but the human one. It appeared that mankind had created a technology beyond his social capabilities to guide it. I became convinced of a long-

I began my preparation for a professional career.

deferred need for substantive improvements in public education
that would help children become the kind of caring, intelligent, rational beings that could live in peace with their fellow
residents on this planet, live in harmony with their natural
environment, and live satisfying personal lives in a technological world.

> Few people at the beginning of the nineteenth cen-
> tury needed an adman to tell them what they want.
>   —JOHN KENNETH GALBRAITH

As I perceived the problem, the most significant step toward
this objective would be improvement in teacher education.
All of the other proposed and welcome educational improvements—smaller classes, more financial support, better books,
buildings, and equipment—would be of limited value unless
there was an accompanying increase in teacher competence.
I learned about and employed a most effective technique for

studying teacher performance and for developing effective programs to produce teacher competence.* The technique is commonly known as the systems approach. Although the process of systematically analyzing and testing each component that went into the teacher education program was a time-consuming enterprise, the results proved to be demonstrably superior to those achieved by traditional teacher education programs. My experience in successfully applying the systems approach to teacher education stimulated me to consider the possibility of improving other human and social conditions through a similar approach.

Man is an incurable systems builder.

The systems approach is not new. Its ultimate achievement to date has been the space program, which has landed man on

* Laurence J. Peter, *Competencies for Teaching,* Vol. 1, *Individual Instruction;* Vol. II, *Classroom Instruction;* Vol. III, *Therapeutic Instruction;* Vol. IV, *Teacher Education,* (Belmont, Calif.: Wadsworth Publishing Company, Inc., *1975*).

the moon, but it has seldom been applied effectively to down-to-earth human problems.

> To condemn technology *in toto* is to forget gardens
> made green by desalinization of sea water, while to
> idealize technology is to forget Hiroshima.
> —STUART CHASE

Because of man's creative nature, he is an incurable systems builder. Throughout his history, he has organized his observations into systems. He has developed systems of rules or laws for social conduct. He has created systems for navigation. He has built systems of roads. He has organized his observations into systems of knowledge that he calls sciences. He has even organized the unknown into systems of belief, worship, and occult studies. All human societies, whether called primitive or civilized, are man-made systems. Our technologies, whether they consist of simple tools and weapons or advanced electronic, communication, and transportation networks, are man-made systems.

Unfortunately, most man-made systems for dealing with social problems developed haphazardly, with little attention to the long-term consequences. Nobody actually planned to pollute the atmosphere. Nobody planned that social welfare would reinforce and increase the problems it was established to eliminate. Nobody planned the population explosion of both newborn and aged as a side effect of improvement in medical treatment. Nobody planned that the ultimate outcome of our abundance would be a state of affluent poverty.

Out in Excelsior Valley farmers still grew the crops that supplied food items for the residents of Excelsior City. A vast array of components was involved in handling and processing these agricultural products. The farmers required seed, feed, machinery, fertilizers, pesticides, and other chemical products to produce their crops. Trucks and railways provided transportation components that moved the farmers' supplies in and

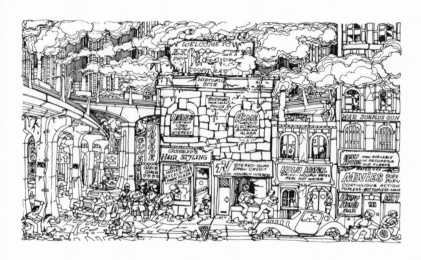

We lived in a state of affluent poverty.

the produce out to wholesale depots. The song of meadowlarks was replaced by the sound of diesel engines, and fumes crowded out the smell of hay at mowing time. In town, at the grimy depot, the farmers' fresh products were processed and eventually delivered to stores and supermarkets, from which they were purchased and then consumed.

> The path of civilization is paved with tin cans.
> —ELBERT HUBBARD

Today, analyzing this process from a systems point of view, it is obvious that many elements are unaccounted for. One of the most obvious discrepancies is the lack of any responsible accountability for waste products generated by the process. Nutrients from the soil are converted into edible plants, some of which are consumed as food, some discarded during processing, some thrown out by the retailers, and some parts— leaves, peelings, and leftovers—become household garbage.

This garbage ends up either in the city dump or in the sewer that empties into Excelsior River and then in turn empties into Excelsior Bay. This is a one-way flow. Agricultural soil in the valley is depleted of organic matter, and the river and bay are overloaded with nitrogen and waste products. A systems analyst would perceive this as a highly organized, sophisticated, *incomplete* system that produces, transports, and sells products, but one that cannot be bothered to employ more than a primitive procedure for handling those elements viewed as nonprofitable. A total systems approach such as the kind found in use where the government is willing to subsidize the planning, or where industry has otherwise found it to be profitable, would account for all elements and would develop the components necessary for returning the nutrients to the soil so that ecological balance is maintained and the total system is nonpolluting.

This concept of recycling occurs naturally where people live closer to the land. In parts of the Old World the same land has been farmed for thousands of years and is still productive because organic matter is returned to the soil from whence it came.

A systems analyst studying the Excelsior Valley agricultural industry would discover that the depletion of humus in the soil permits the chemical fertilizers to be leached through the soil into the river. This results in the farmers requiring more and more chemical fertilizers, most of which are supplied by Polyglot Chemical Corp., located further upstream on the banks of Excelsior Lake. The chemical and industrial waste from Polyglot flow into Excelsior Lake and then into the river where they are joined by the agricultural pollutants that eventually combine with the sewage from the city to produce a stinking, combustible mixture of miasmic methane and other gases. On several occasions the surface of the river has caught fire, and one fire recently destroyed the Upper Excelsior River Bridge. Vessels operating on this busy waterway contribute further to the contamination. Most of the fish have died, and the river long ago lost its utility for recreation purposes. It still, of course, serves as the city's water supply. While this was happening, our myopic Mayor C. Nyle continued to campaign for increased industrialization of the Excelsior River Basin.

A systems analyst would examine all of the components of the agricultural products industry and find that pesticides, which had been originally used with discretion and precision in the days of hand application, are now distributed freely and in great volume by mechanical applicators and released over vast green areas from the air. Even when the pesticides are effective, they also destroy the beneficent insects and other predators that are the natural enemies of the crop-damaging insects. Winds carry the pesticides beyond their target areas, poisoning wild and domestic animals. Farm workers in distant fields may develop symptoms of pesticide poisoning. The pesticides that are not leached by the rain deep into the soil are washed into the river. When they reach the ocean they further contaminate the fish that have not already succumbed to the discharge from Polyglot Chemical or the effluent from one of Excelsior Valley's leading industries, Mercury Paper Mills, on which much of the town's livelihood depends. Sea birds that feed on the fish eventually expire or produce defective eggs that will not hatch, a fate not unlike the land birds that consume the insects poisoned by the pesticides. People who eat the contaminated fish accumulate the pesticide in their body tissue, as do the infant offspring who drink the milk from the cows that graze on grass contaminated by the pesticide.

A systems analyst would examine the handling of the produce as it leaves the farm. He would find that it is bulk loaded during its trip to the wholesaler. It leaves the wholesaler in convenient, nonreturnable cardboard cartons manufactured by Mercury Paper Mills. The wood pulp is obtained from logs supplied by Clear Cut Logging Co. These cartons eventually end up at the city dump. In the market, the shopper selects the best-looking vegetables and fruit and puts them into plastic bags, a by-product of Beachslic Petroleum. At the checkout, the packaged products and plastic bags are placed in a paper sack, another product of Mercury Mills. In the home, all of these containers go into the garbage.

The crucial problem with this system is that it does not feed back into the land the ingredients it has removed. Every escalation of productivity, every improvement of this incomplete system ultimately is disastrous. The precious few inches of topsoil—upon which life depends—is polluted so the vicious cycles of environmental degradation proliferate.

This one-way system consists of components earnestly developed by farmers, loggers, financiers, industrialists, chemists, truckers, merchandisers, advertisers and consumers, each escalating their contributions to the system in hit-or-miss and stopgap attempts to increase production, make more money, or save housework.

> If the blind lead the blind, both shall fall into the ditch.
>
> —MATT. 15: 14

To counter some of the more immediately devastating effects of technology, a number of laws have been enacted to limit the amount of industrial waste discharged into the river, the amount of smoke released into the atmosphere, and the amount of mercury and other poisons permitted in the food we eat. These laws, even when enforced, only slow down the environmental degradation. They do not change the direction of the one-way system leading ultimately to disaster.

> The best laid schemes o' mice and men
> Gang aft a-gley.
>
> —ROBERT BURNS

In contrast to the hit-or-miss method, the systems approach seeks to arrange all the components of a system to work in

Produce and products terminated in pollution (Goods In—Garbage Out).

The vicious cycles of environmental degredation proliferate.

harmonious, interrelated cooperation. It is not a magical solution, nor is it a new solution. What is new is the degree of development of the skills of systems analysts in dealing with large-scale problems. The essence of the approach is still only common sense and logic applied realistically and consistently. Although its core is common sense, the method requires that this be enhanced by large quantities of detailed and accurate knowledge, along with the intellectual discipline to bring that knowledge to bear on the problem. Nature is not easily duplicated by man.

The systems approach will not provide immediate answers to all problems. Even if outstanding systems teams were established, errors would be made as a result of a lack of *correct* information. The systems approach, however, consists of analysis and decision-making based on the firm resolve to be complete, orderly, logical, and accurate. Through persistent application of the total systems approach, errors are corrected and harmony restored.

The Peter Plan is based upon our ability to apply systems dynamics to the major problems facing mankind. The Peter Plan is not intended to achieve the perfection of a utopian society, but it is a process whereby harmonious relationships with our environment and our fellow inhabitants of this planet may be achieved. The Peter Plan is not a static but a dynamic process by which individuals and society can move forward to a higher quality of life, rather than to higher and higher levels of peril.

Whether or not we will have systems is not the question. We will have systems, because it is our nature to create systems. Rather, the question is, shall we have piecemeal systems based on random components that escalate us toward incompetence, or shall we have a systems approach that utilizes our total knowledge—along with our instincts for survival and what we know is good—to integrate our social and humanistic goals with our technological achievements and ecological

needs? If we choose the latter, man's greatest age of achievement lies ahead.

> There is a past which is gone forever, but there is a
> future which is still our own.
>
> —F. W. ROBERTSON

CHAPTER II

Pathology

I believe that order is better than chaos, creation
better than destruction. I prefer gentleness to violence, forgiveness to vendetta. On the whole I think
that knowledge is preferable to ignorance, and I
am sure that human sympathy is more valuable
than ideology . . . in spite of the recent triumphs
of science, men haven't changed much in the last
2,000 years, and in consequence we must still try
to learn from history. History is ourselves.
                                    —KENNETH CLARK

As a young man I had a layman's familiarity with the difficulties confronting Excelsior City and more than average curiosity about solutions. The years passed and I became aware
of the complexity and interrelatedness of these problems. In
my attempt to understand, I increased my reading in a wide
range of subjects, including conservation, population, sociology, economics, crime, city planning, and history.

From the first permanent settlement of European immi-
grants in America at Jamestown in the beginning of the seventeenth century, it took about one century to settle the area
between the Atlantic Ocean and the Allegheny Mountains,
another century to populate the land to the Mississippi, and
most of the last century before the frontier had disappeared.
The pioneer met the challenge of the frontier by clearing the

I increased my reading in a wide range of related subjects.

land, building the railways, killing the buffalo, fighting the Indians, and generally plundering the natural resources. Although by 1900 the invaders had subdued the native peoples and conquered the land, the frontier mentality persisted.

> To follow foolish precedents, and wink
> With both our eyes is easier than to think.
> —WILLIAM COWPER

The first seventy-five years of this century have been witness to perpetuation of growth and greed, with almost universal indifference to any consequence other than mere profit. We have consistently failed to perceive the whole picture and how to maintain a viable balance between the works of man and ways and wisdom of nature. The period from the closing of the frontier to the present is testimony to failure through fragmentation.

Around the turn of the century Excelsior Valley bore some

scars of exploitation of its natural resources. Clear Cut Logging Co. had begun strip mining, but the river still flowed clear and provided recreation. Families still swam, picnicked, and fished along the shores.

Man increased the ways in which he could work his will on nature. The methods that drew the shortest lines to the highest profits were the greatest despoilers. Now in 1975, Excelsior Valley is a scarred and sullen witness to the folly of false profits.

> There is no fortress so strong that money cannot take it.
> —CICERO

And in the world beyond Excelsior County, vast areas of the planet are covered with a yellowish haze of smog. The pollutants are concentrated over the cities, where the people are trapped in the thickening air.

In Japan, the schoolchildren are bussed from the industrial cities so that they can see what clear air looks and feels like.

In Italy, during the worst of the Milan winter smog season, travelers are advised to take the train rather than the plane, because frequently pollution causes such poor visibility that the planes cannot land.

Beside the grandest boulevard in Mexico City, the Paseo de la Reforma, the flowering plants die of air pollution and must be replaced every two months.

> Forty million pounds of dog dung are deposited annually on the streets of New York City.
> —RAYMOND HULL

Along a busy Los Angeles boulevard, where real plants cannot survive, plastic ferns and trees beckon with their sun-faded artificial arms to passing drivers, who do not know whether to snicker or to avert their eyes.

The San Bernardino National Forest, one of California's

most beautiful recreational mountain areas, will be a desert within twenty-five years, at the rate that smog is killing the Jeffrey and ponderosa pines.

In London, a woman awakens from a nightmare, dreaming she is being smothered, and then lies quietly listening to her child wheeze with pollution-induced asthma.

In Germany, a 406-year-old village, Knapsack, has the dubious honor of being the first town in the history of civilization to be officially declared uninhabitable because of air pollution. Knapsack is the second largest phosphate producer in the world, but fumes from the phosphate plant have forced the residents to move away and their houses have been demolished. The town of Knapsack has disappeared.

> I hate the pollyanna pest who says that all is for
> the best.
>   —F. P. ADAMS

Vast areas of the Atlantic Ocean are befouled by massive amounts of oil and plastics. Oil dumped by tankers steaming down the west coast of Africa ends up in an 850,000 square-mile area along the U.S. East Coast and the Caribbean. Thick, sludgy clumps about the size of a human fist extrude like spaghetti through fishing nets.

It was not an easy matter for me to accept the degree to which the earth's environment was worsening. When I was a boy in school, I was taught that technology was synonymous with progress. I believed in efficiency. America was the land of efficiency, and its scientific know-how was an inspiration to the rest of the world.

> What is the new loyalty? It is, above all, confor-
> mity. It is the uncritical and unquestioning accep-
> tance of America as it is.
>   —HENRY STEELE COMMAGER

America has long pointed with great pride to its unparalleled economic growth and achievement. Now this achieve-

Thick sludgy globs of oil extruded through fishing nets.

ment is under indictment by those who see it as preoccupation with bigness and economic power at the expense of the quality of life. Our recent environmental and social crises challenge our traditional and fundamental American assumption that economic growth is a good thing per se. Our traditional belief in the value of growth in all areas is based on the concept that bigger is better, and therefore we can measure our overall progress as a nation by our tabulation of our total production—GNP (gross national product). It is concerned only with quantity. Every plane that crashes raises the GNP and thereby, statistically, raises the standard of living. The cost of replacing the plane, invstigating the crash, treating the survivors, and burying the dead all help to escalate the GNP. And on a smaller scale, every auto crash contributes to the GNP, and so does the production of tobacco, the manufacture of cigarettes, the treatment of victims of lung cancer, and the building of caskets for those who succumb to the disease.

Every auto crash contributes to the GNP.

The increasing GNP represents more of something. It could be more production, a declining quality of goods and services, a grossly deteriorating environment, and escalation of the pathological side-effects of growth for growth's sake.

> When you get there there isn't any there there.
> —GERTRUDE STEIN

The GNP is not a measure of the quality of life but merely the total cost of goods and services. It is like a cost-plus contract that pays a bonus for inefficiency, delays, waste, redundancy, breakdowns, and short-lived, throwaway products. Every business conspiracy to raise prices, every employee strike, every product with built-in obsolescence, every unnecessary or obsolete weapon manufactured, and every war causes the GNP to go up. The GNP could stand for Gross National Pathology.

The Gross National Product does not account for love,

beauty, nature's wonders, clean air, pure water, peace of mind, quiet, privacy, happiness, or many other aspects of the quality of life that cannot be totaled at the national checkout counter.

> Economic growth is not only unnecessary, but ruinous.
>
> —ALEXANDER SOLZHENITSYN

In analyzing and coming to grips with these facts, I tried to retrace the development of my growing disillusionment with the traditional escalatory way of life. My memories came to me in a disconnected pattern that made little sense—at first.

> The certainties of one age are the problems of the next.
>
> —R. H. TAWNEY

I recalled my economics instructor, Professor D. Kaye, saying, "If power, automobile production, and water consumption are escalating faster than population, then it is reasonable to assume that the standard of living is improving."

At Excelsior College I sat on an old oak bench in Founder's Hall listening to every word of an eloquent speech in which Professor D. Kaye defended his proposition that escalation of the GNP, the world over, would lead to universal material well-being. He said, "City dwellers in the advanced countries have the most and best housing, schools, transportation, and other services. Progress is synonymous with escalation of technological efficiency and economic growth. The advanced nations must help the underdeveloped nations in escalating their production. When they have more people, more and faster planes, more automobiles, more washing machines, and more powerful weapons, they will have a higher standard of living as well as the military capability to defend their way of life."

My memory of D. Kaye's lecture was interrupted by a scene in which my biology instructor, Professor A. Lyrte, demonstrated the effects of overpopulation. For his first experiment

*I listened to Professor D. Kaye's eloquent explanation
of his GNP theories.*

he placed two flies, along with some food, in a bottle. In a
few days the bottle contained a multitude of healthy, active
flies. During the next few days the overcrowding and their
own effluence caused an increased death rate, and then the
population dropped suddenly to zero. A Lyrte believed that
escalation of human population, or of environmentally destructive technology, was a one-way street that eventually
would lead to destruction of all mankind and its environment.

Now I realize what I should have said to them. "You are
both wrong. D. Kaye, your patriotic stance and obsolete
economic theories ignore the fact that we live on a finite
sphere. Our resources are limited to what we have right here.
A. Lyrte, you have a point, but we don't live in a bottle.
We can change our environment. Sure, we have made a mess
of some things, but we have the technical know-how to make
things work. Look at our plumbing, railways, postal system,
planes, telephones, vending machines . . . well, perhaps not

The population dropped suddenly to zero.

vending machines. Here more than anywhere else, technology provides more individuals with the benefits of the automobile, television, computers, convenience foods, nonreturnable bottles, deodorants, plastics, cyclamates, psychotropic drugs, hormone-treated beef."

> I think we must save America from the missionary idea that you must get the whole world on the American way of life. That is really a big world danger.
>
> —GUNNAR MYRDAL

I recalled reading that the Chicago Transit Authority had opened a new 5.2-mile subway line that suffered four derailments and one collision during its first few days in operation. More than forty persons were injured. Chicago had created transportation history that—though ranking behind the voyage of the *Titanic* and the landing of the *Hindenburg* in dramatic impact—added immeasurably to the GNP.

Excelsior City's low-income and welfare families needed housing. With characteristic foresight the civic government sponsored a project concentrating these underprivileged groups in a huge low-cost, high-rise project. This resulted in a local overload of unskilled persons in Excelsior Towers. These people are now further from the mainstream of city life. There are no jobs within commuting distance of the housing project so the residents are unable to find jobs. The welfare roles continue to grow and the crime rate escalates.

The House Armed Services Subcommittee asked the Pentagon for one copy of each of its standard forms. They received 11,916 different forms.

> Military intelligence is a contradiction in terms.
> —GROUCHO MARX

Nuclear bombs are unusable weapons. The object of having them is to keep others from using theirs. At the present proliferation rate, the chance of an all-out nuclear disaster increases 2 percent per year. By the year 2000, chances will be 50-50.

> You can't say civilization don't advance, however,
> for in every war they kill you in a new way.
> —WILL ROGERS

A recession was feared, so the President declared a new missile gap and the Pentagon dispensed more defense contracts. More and more citizens became dependent on the defense establishment and society's ability to solve nonmilitary problems was further depleted.

> Ours is a world of nuclear giants and ethical infants.
> —GENERAL OMAR BRADLEY

The Soviet Union and the United States have stockpiled

between them the explosive power of 15 tons of TNT for every man, woman, and child on this earth. Even the poor are affluent in destructive power.

> More and more, the choice for the world's peoples
> is between world warriors or world citizens.
> —Norman Cousins

In the U.S. the demand for electric power is doubling every ten years. Most of this power is derived from rapidly diminishing reserves of domestic fossil fuels and foreign imports of petroleum. The demand for oil and the escalation of oil imports has made the U.S. one of the most dependent countries in the world.

World population is growing by 70 million persons every year and the rate is still accelerating. The power of the population explosion is greater than the power of the earth to produce sustenance. Man is taking fresh water out of the ground twice as fast as natural processes are replacing it. Each year 10 million new cars are built, and each car burns fossil fuel, poisons the air, grinds rubber tires into dust, and wears asbestos brakes into acrid powder. All Hail, GNP!

> As the carpet of "increased choice" is being un-
> rolled before us by the foot, it is simultaneously
> being rolled up behind us by the yard.
> —Ezra J. Mishan

If all this continues, what kind of ecological time bomb am I handing my children? This is the pathology of our way of life: We continue to believe that escalation is progress when in fact much of our escalation does not and cannot produce progress. There is public bafflement, frustration, and outrage because the bureaus of government appear to be purposeless and are themselves victims of the escalation syndrome. Government institutions bear promising titles. The Department of Health, Education and Welfare (HEW) receives a large measure of support, but health services are so unevenly distributed and medical costs are so high that the average citizen lives in terror of becoming ill. Financial support for education in some school districts is neglected to the point that schools are closing, and many pupils attending those schools that remain open are receiving such inadequate instruction that they fail to learn. Johnny can't read and Jill comes tumbling after. Welfare promises alleviation of many ills of our society, but fails to fulfill its promise, while the lion's share of the budget is devoured by administration.

> This country, with its institutions, belongs to the people who inhibit it.
>
> —EDGAR A. SHOAFF

Escalation without progress is not only a monopoly of profit-making bureaucracies. Soviet Russia has polluted the Caspian Sea as diligently as America has destroyed Lake Erie. The idea that more equals better seems to be universal.

> If misery loves company the U.S. and U.S.S.R. should adore each other.
>
> —JAMES F. MAGARY

A strong belief in escalation of personnel, money, or materials as the solution to problems results in more activity but no real progress. According to the tenets of our conventional wisdom, the solution to bumper-to-bumper traffic is to escalate highway construction. We end up by paving more of the land with flat monuments to our stupidity and with still bigger traffic jams.

> Neither a wise man nor a brave man lies down on the tracks of history to wait for the train of the future to run over him.
>
> —DWIGHT D. EISENHOWER

We will get richer and richer in dirtier and dirtier communities. The wealthiest among us will become the gods living on Mt. Trashmore, while the poor grovel around the base of the garbage heap. In the name of progress we continue to escalate the destruction of our planet as a place for human life. But we will not be so fortunate as the bird that fouled its own nest and then moved on. We are fouling the only home we have.

> Those who cannot remember the past are condemned to repeat it.
>
> —GEORGE SANTAYANA

CHAPTER III

Paradox

How quaint the ways of Paradox!
At common sense she gaily mocks.
—W. S. GILBERT

WHILE I was growing up in Excelsior City, I accepted the traditional concepts. My disenchantment has been neither a gradual process nor an abrupt revelation. As I look back, it seems that I have been confronted by a series of contradictions that have challenged my conventional ideas.

I keep reading between the lies.
—GOODMAN ACE

Some time ago an appliance salesman was trying to convince me that I needed a new refrigerator. He described a new feature that my old refrigerator lacked—a thermal butter box. His sales pitch caused me to question the conventional concept of technological progress. It is cold outside, so I insulate and heat my house. I have a refrigerator to protect my food from the warmth in my house. Now I am told that I need a thermal butter box unit in my refrigerator to keep my butter warm.

A society that expands production by expanding wants can never have a large margin available over seeming need.
—JOHN KENNETH GALBRAITH

45

I need a thermal butter box?

At a time when nothing seems to work—the mail is late, the railroads are bankrupt, fuel is scarce, and the government is seemingly helpless to cope—I am offered a better life through a new gadget, a thermal butter box. Somehow this incident stimulated me to direct my attention to things we needed far more than a thermal unit to keep our butter warm.

> Men become civilized, not in proportion to their
> willingness to believe, but in proportion to their
> readiness to doubt.
>
> —H. L. MENCKEN

We need to make some big adjustments in our traditional values if we humans now inhabiting this planet are going to save our species from a rude and unpleasant future. The threat is a serious one. If we are not doomed, those who survive will be pollution-resistant mutations—human equivalents to the scavenger carp that lurk in Lake Erie's fetid depths, living off poison and decay.

> We have met the enemy and they are us.
> —POGO (WALT KELLY)

Our national hunger for continuous growth and for being Number One in everything is as outdated as ritual sacrifices. Getting to the top and staying there is more valued by modern man than the more challenging pursuit of keeping it all together for human survival. We are terrified that we might have to give up any of the so-called benefits of progress, even to live. Most of my acquaintances, ostrich-like, would rather not discuss survival. They would prefer to keep the conversation lighthearted. If I want a serious conversation they would rather discuss television, tennis, or football. It is their way of expressing the wish that the problems related to humanity's future would go away.

> It is not so important to be serious as it is to be
> serious about important things.
> —ROBERT M. HUTCHINS

We face an ecological crisis because we are out of harmony with nature's ways of survival. We take from nature that which cannot be replaced and create waste that cannot be absorbed by natural cycles. Common sense tells us that *infinite growth* cannot be sustained by *finite resources*.

> Common sense in an uncommon degree is what the
> world calls wisdom.
> —SAMUEL TAYLOR COLERIDGE

We are beginning to understand that our old ideas of prosperity may have distracted us from the realities of global catastrophe. Will we continue to offer extraordinary resistance to the evidence? Will we learn to play the game of life not to escalate but to survive, or, so long as we can manage to draw a breath, will we opt for short-term prosperity?

Callous greed grows pious very fast.
                              —LILLIAN HELLMAN

The answers to these questions depend upon the nature of the human species. Is mankind essentially good, infinitely corruptible, perfectible, or somewhat modifiable? In the answers to these questions we will find the prospect for continued human existence on the planet.

> One of the weaknesses of our age is our apparent
> inability to distinguish our needs from our greeds.
>   —DON ROBINSON

The human species has never been very successful in controlling the destruction of community property. We have laws to prevent rape, robbery, and traffic violations, but we have few to keep us from despoiling our communal planet. The inadequacy of our laws to protect the world in which we live is characteristic of self-defeating human behavior. We have not yet developed the intelligence to interpret the behavior of global systems. Human judgment and intuition tend to look only to the immediate past for the causes of problems.

> Perhaps we are wise, less selfish and more far-
> seeing than we were 200 years ago. But we are still
> imperfectly all these good things, and since the
> turn of the century it has been remarked that
> neither wisdom nor virtue has increased as rapidly
> as the need for both.
>   —J. W. KRUTCH

The government drains wetlands so farmers can grow more crops while it pays farmers to let fertile cropland lie idle. If it were only money against money it would be the height of foolishness, but compounding this absurd, wasteful felony is the disturbing fact that it also destroys irreplaceable wildlife habitat. Furthermore, draining the wetlands spoils the natural means of water retention, so that the project becomes counterproductive, causing a need for further flood control measures.

Is our environment to be handed over to ceaseless,
unthinking development by those who think only of
what it could yield to them today? . . . There's a
planet who needs your help.

—GARRETT DE BELL

Politicians have been successful in persuading citizens that
welfare is a major financial problem, but they fail to mention
the fact that federal crop subsidy programs cost taxpayers
more than all the federal, state, and local welfare programs
combined. In a recent year, five hundred large growers in
California's Imperial Valley received $12 million in farm
subsidies—or $24,000 each. Meanwhile, 10,000 poor, land-
less residents of the valley received less than $8 million in
welfare payments—or $800 each. Welfare for the rich may
be more of a financial burden than welfare for the poor.

We can have democracy in the country or we can
have great wealth concentrated in the hands of a
few, but we can't have both.

—LOUIS D. BRANDEIS

Somewhere in our history we moved slowly from a government of the people to a government by vast bureaucracies.
Within the mazes of the federal government there are huge
empires removed as far from the processes of elective representative government as were the courts of Nero or Ivan the
Terrible. Of all the bureaucracies that have a stranglehold on
American life, the Pentagon takes first place. The military has
maneuvered the elected representatives into waging war with
distant countries that pose no threat to America. The strength
of the Pentagon is measured in part by the billions of dollars
it commands. Its self-perpetuating character exercises a powerful impact on the public mind. Its public relations men, and
most of the mass media, voice the causes of the military-
industrial complex, so that the majority of us are relentlessly
pushed in the direction that the Pentagon bureaucracy wishes.

It has become routine to increase the military budget by billions while cutting back on education, health, and model-city programs. The only reassurance offered by our leaders is the treacherous security of building more nuclear weapons than the Communists, when common sense tells us there will be no scorekeeper around to record the desolate fact of whose weapon superiority won the final battle. The bomb has not made war impossible—only victory.

> In the councils of government, we must guard against the requisition of unwarranted influence, whether sought or unsought, by the military-industrial complex.
>
> —DWIGHT D. EISENHOWER

When I was a boy in school I asked questions about mankind's mindless aggression and self-destructive behavior. I was told that it was human nature to be that way. Later I was told that man is no more than an animal among animals, a

There will be no scorekeeper.

naked ape dominated by his own savage biology and his killer instincts. This cynical and overly pessimistic view of mankind gained popularity as a rationalization for the absurdity of human behavior. The killing of one's own kind is almost unheard of in the animal kingdom. The killers of the animal world are predators who only kill to eat. The great apes are shy, unaggressive, almost exclusively vegetarian, and live cooperatively in societies or groups of one hundred or less.

The great apes live cooperatively.

The human animal is a species whose biologically inherited behavior can be modified by society, which is in turn a human creation. The great variety of different cultures created by man sets him apart from apes and other animal species. If humans were innately aggressive, all mankind would inevitably be aggressive in highly predictable standard behavior. Some societies are aggressive and some are nonviolent. Human aggression is expressed in widely varying ways, ranging from debate, verbal insults, and threats, to attempts at physical dominance in hand-to-hand combat or warfare. Physical dominance may be expressed in weight-lifting or other tests of strength. Skill is expressed in boxing and wrestling conducted within a set of rules. Symbolic battles are waged between opposing teams on the football field. Aggression may be expressed in more highly symbolic ways such as playing chess, checkers, cards, and other competitive games. There is a great difference between human behavior and the reflexive and highly stereotyped aggressive responses made by lower animals. The human aggressive response is shaped by the particular culture in which the individual lives, rather than by instinct.

> When a man wants to murder a tiger he calls it sport; when the tiger wants to murder him he calls it ferocity.
> —G. B. SHAW

Apologists for modern man's arrogant behavior have misinterpreted the idea of evolution through survival of the fittest. They have taken it to mean that life is a free-for-all struggle in which fitness is equated with aggression by tooth and claw. Survival of a species is not the result of aggression to achieve immediate advantage. It is *adaptation to achieve interdependence* with others. Interdependence in nature has evolved because it confers mutual benefits on the participants.

> One touch of Darwin makes the whole world kin.
> —G. B. SHAW

As a boy I visited a number of Indian villages along the southern coast of British Columbia and became acquainted with some members of the Salish, Kwakiutl, and Haida tribes. I was fascinated by their tales of olden days when tribal life was free of the white man's law and religion. Although the Indian potlatch had been outlawed by the Canadian government in 1884, back in the 1920s, when I visited their villages, the potlatch was still being celebrated as a colorful and ritual-

istic festival, but without its earlier purpose. The true potlatch
of old was given by a Chief for his own and neighboring clans.
It was a great social event intended to enhance his reputation
and increase the security of his clan for future generations.
It was traditional for the Indian to rely in almost all of his
undertakings on the help of his friends. It was understood that
he would pay them for the help at a later date. The potlatch
was the public performance of the contracting for, and pay-
ment of, these obligations. Outwardly, the potlatch followed
a similar pattern along the entire British Columbia coast. A
clan prepared for a potlatch for several years by gathering
vast stores of food, blankets, art objects, and other articles
intended as gifts. The Chief then sent out invitations.

The chief sent out invitations to the potlatch.

The guests, in their best festive attire, usually arrived by
canoe and made a ceremonial entrance singing a peace song.
Welcoming dances were performed, and then the feasting
began. Presents were distributed each day. The status of the

Chief and his clan depended in large meaure on how much he gave away. This constituted a form of social security, because the guest Chiefs and clans were obligated to return the favor. Thus, the Chief who gave away the most had the most coming to him at a later potlatch, or after his death, the obligation was due his successor. As part of the potlatch ceremony, an elaborate totem pole was erected to stand as a witness and a validation of what had taken place. This Indian culture granted social status on the basis of giving rather than receiving. It reduced long-term hoarding of wealth and established bonds of peaceful cooperation between the clans.

> And where are the others that might have stood
> Side by your side in the common good?
> —MAURICE OGDEN

One of modern man's explanations for his aggressions is his inherent territoriality—a popular theory that man's primary motivation stems from a biological urge to defend an area against intruders. Examination of the evidence does not support the idea that it is universal, automatic, or imperative in man's nature to defend territory. Primitive peoples who live by hunting animals and gathering natural vegetation are the least territorial of human groups. In Africa there are many areas in which tribes of different ethnic heritage live harmoniously in the same territory, deriving sustenance from the same environment in different ways.

> There is no conflict between liberty and safety.
> We will have both or neither.
> —RAMSEY CLARK

The nomadic Eskimos of the American Arctic live in clans or extended families, with no permanent associations to particular territory. Being almost completely isolated from other cultures, they have developed their own to suit their particular habitat. Security for the Eskimo depends not on territory but

on those from whom one can freely request support and in
turn have it demanded of him. This sense of collective responsibility, loyalty, and obligation to one's clan is the basis
of the social organization. Each individual owns his own
personal clothing and tools, but shelter and food are held in
common.

Although there are no chiefs or formal arbiters of disputes,
problems are resolved without resorting to bloodshed. Public
opinion and public ridicule are the main means of maintaining
order. Men may wrestle to settle a dispute or have a song
duel, in which, at a public gathering, the two rivals voice
their quarrel by insulting each other in extemporaneous song.

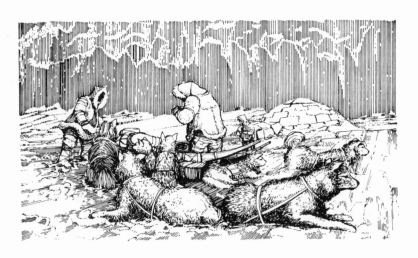

The Eskimos' security did not depend on territory.

Modern man tends to believe that competition is the driving
force behind progress, but this belief does not stand up to close
scrutiny. Competition has no inherent virtue. There is plenty
of competition in organized crime. Competition between na-

tions has resulted in development of horrendous weapons. Competition can be the motivating force to produce the best or the worst.

> I still remember the effect I produced on a small group of Galla tribesmen massed around a man in black clothes. I dropped an aerial torpedo right in the center, and the group opened up like a flowering rose. It was most entertaining.
>
> —VITTORIO MUSSOLINI

The idea that humans evolved through relentless competition with each other is false. Because our own games are so highly competitive, we think all human beings are born competitors, but the games of many cultures are not. The Tangu people of New Guinea play a popular game, taketak, which consists of throwing a spinning top into groups of stakes driven into the ground. Each of two teams of players tries to touch as many stakes with their tops as possible. The participants play not to win but to draw. The game goes on until an exact draw is achieved. Taketak expresses a basic value in Tangu culture—the concept of moral equivalency, which is also reflected in the precise sharing of food among the people.

An outstanding example of nonviolence is found in the Semai, a farming people of Malaya. Their children are never punished physically and rarely see any form of violence, so have no model of aggression to emulate. If adults become angry they usually confine themselves to voicing insults. Murder is unknown among the Semai. Sometimes, when frustrated, they throw their own belongings around, but they use caution so as not to hurt anyone. Even this degree of violence is disapproved of, because throwing things might scare people.

There are so many examples of individual, group, and tribal nonviolence that I cannot but conclude that the theorists who attribute civilized man's violence and war-making to

Tangu people share food equally.

human nature, inborn territoriality, and killer instinct are rationalizing to justify modern man's senseless aggression.

> Truly man is king of beasts for his brutality exceeds theirs.

> —LEONARDO DA VINCI

Individual behavior within a particular culture lends further credence to the concept of human variability. One scientist devotes his life to raising the yield of agricultural crops to help feed the peoples of the world, while another devotes his efforts to developing weapons for warfare. One author dedicates his time and talent to writing about peace, love, and understanding between the peoples of the world, while another writes hate literature. One politician fights for honest government and justice for all, while another practices extortion and subverts justice to enhance his power. One citizen practices conservation and accepts responsibility for protecting the environment, while another heedlessly litters and destroys his natural surroundings. One individual works for consumer protection, while another works for organized crime. And so on.

> Ah, how unjust to nature and himself
> Is thoughtless, thankless, inconsistent man!
> —EDWARD YOUNG

The human species is a paradox not because it is inherently good or evil, but because biologically, socially, and ethically, it has the most adaptable behavior of all living organisms. During the formative years a child learns its attitudes and behavior patterns from its parents, teachers, and other cultural influences. Without instruction the child would not even consider going thousands of miles across an ocean to drop bombs on peasant villages and farms. By shaming those who find killing in defense of their country's "honor" morally repugnant, by political maneuvering to make the public feel that their territory will be threatened, and by draft laws, individuals are conditioned to accept warfare as a justifiable aggressive act. Similarly, a culture based on nonviolence produces individuals with entirely different behavior patterns. Within certain genetic limitations, each human being is a product of his culture and his unique creative and mental powers. It is with these powers that he can change his behavior and ultimately his society.

> The hardest thing to learn in life is which bridge to
> cross and which to burn.
> —DAVID RUSSELL

Unique as each individual is, we are nevertheless all programmed genetically to need clean air, unpolluted water, and uncontaminated food. To survive in a healthy state means simply allowing our bodies to react in the ways that 100 million years of evolution have equipped us to function. In this way nature imposes limitations on individual freedom. In other words, we are not free to breathe foul air, drink polluted water, or eat poisoned food.

> The control man has secured over nature has far outrun his control over himself.
>
> —ERNEST JONES

Freedom implies the right to make choices, but we are not free to choose to break the laws of the land. Penalties are imposed if we make that choice. We have freedom to be creative and fulfill our unique individuality, but we do not have freedom to impose our will on our environment in violation of natural laws. The penalty for violation of the environment is often paid for later by the innocent bystander, rather than by the perpetrator of the crime. This means, unfortunately, that the natural penalty need not deter the offender.

> The world is a paradox of technological progressiveness and social primitivism.
>
> —SIMON RAMO

If we fail to understand the nature of freedom, this most vital, human, and precious possession, we may destroy its source—our habitat. We will never build a spaceship as beautiful as earth, never one so suited to our needs, never one with such potential for our true progress toward fulfillment of our highest humanity.

> The danger of the past was that men became slaves. The danger of the future is that men may become robots.
>
> —ERICH FROMM

It is the paradox of modern man that he has the technology to make long-range predictions but continues to behave in the present with regard for little more than short-term results.

Each year new animals are added to the list of endangered or extinct species. Man, in haughty disregard of the facts, thinks he can escape joining the list.

> We must also avoid the impulse to live only for today, plundering, for our own ease and convenience, the precious resources of tomorrow.
> —DWIGHT D. EISENHOWER

"Dr. Peter, you've forgotten to include man on your list of endangered species."

We have come to the crossroads. We may continue along the road of our aggressive acts against nature, or we may choose to develop systems that are compatible with survival. It is exciting to consider the possible outcomes of these two courses. If we continue to develop our technology without wisdom or prudence, our servant may prove to be our executioner. If we try to change direction we had better know where we are going or it could be from pan to fire. Fortunately, it is possible to visualize the future. We can predict the results of proposed changes in our behavior, society, and environment and foresee their outcome. The Peter Planet is based on my speculations about what the world would be like if we use our present knowledge and technology in the interest of survival of the human species.

I'm afraid of the dark and suspicious of the light.
—WOODY ALLEN

Before we can explore the future of the planet, there are some fundamental things that engage our interest. Although the earth still seems very big to most of us—it is 25,000 miles in circumference and its atmosphere reaches out 600 miles into space—we and other creatures and plants live in a very thin layer that girdles the earth. This layer is called the biosphere (*bio* means life), because within it is found all known earthly life. To say that the biosphere is very thin is not to exaggerate. Except for a few floating spores and bacteria, life occurs only within five miles of the earth's surface, and humans, animals, birds, and plants live in only the first ten thousand feet above sea level. Some life forms are found at all the depths of the ocean, but most marine life exists in the upper five hundred feet. Within this thin layer of the biosphere, the air circulates and water is used over and over by the earth's living organisms. The air you breathe is found only in a narrow layer close to earth, but it need never run out. Our atmosphere has a marvelous self-cleaning system. As long as the system is not overloaded, winds and shifting air masses disperse smoke and dust. In time the solid particles floating in the air settle or are washed out of the air by rain or snow.

Our atmosphere is a mixture of gases. The mixture of nitrogen and oxygen, along with minute quantities of such gases as argon, carbon dioxide, and helium, is maintained with perfect precision by plants, animals, and bacteria, which use and feed back the gases at the appropriate rates. This is a complete system, a balanced cycle in which nothing is wasted and everything is accounted for.

This atmospheric system provides a model for the kind of system man must create. For example, carbon dioxide forms about one part in each 3000 parts of air. As humans and other animals breathe they use up oxygen and exhale carbon dioxide, but plants take in carbon dioxide and give off oxygen so that a balance is maintained.

Lightning releases atmospheric nitrogen so that rain can carry it to earth where it nourishes plants. The plants, in turn, are consumed by animals or the plants grow to fruition and decay. The decaying plants and animal excrement are acted upon by bacteria that release the nitrogen for use by other plants or back into the air. Another cycle is complete.

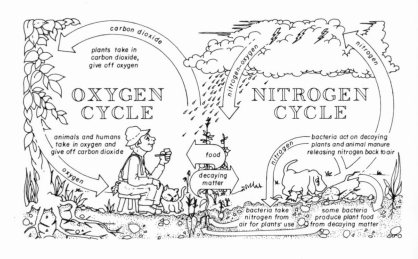

Nature provides a model for the systems man must create.

As long as these natural systems are unimpeded they are self-regulating and continuous. Within the self-cleaning capacity of the system, excess ozone, smoke, and other pollutants are removed so as to maintain clean air. If man increases the input of pollution over the output of purified air, the natural cycle is impaired. Poison gases remain in the atmosphere and clouds of floating filth hang permanently overhead.

> There are people into whose heads it never enters
> to conceive of any better state of society than that
> which now exists.
> —HENRY GEORGE

To survive, man-made systems will have to be as complete as natural cycles and as compatible with nature; that is, they must not overload the capacity of the natural systems. By employing our technology and knowledge of natural systems, we could begin to build a human environment and society in which real human progress could prosper indefinitely. Looking beyond our present difficulties can be an amusing exercise, even informative. It is a way of looking backward so we can move forward. What would our planet be like fifteen years from now if we made the choice today to use our rational powers and our present knowledge of systems dynamics? Let us take a walk around the Peter Planet of 1990.

> He who will not reason, is a bigot; he who cannot
> is a fool; and he who dares not is a slave.
> —SIR WILLIAM DRUMMOND

PART TWO

The Peter Planet

I hold that man is in the right who is most closely
in league with the future.

—Henrik Ibsen

CHAPTER IV

Power

We travel together, passengers on a little space
ship, dependent on its vulnerable resources of air
and soil; all committed for our safety to its security
and peace; preserved from annihilation only by the
work, the care and, I will say, the love we give our
fragile craft.

—ADLAI STEVENSON

In 1990 I could still recognize many of the old familiar land-
marks of Excelsior City. The City Hall, Post Office, Court-
house, and Civic Auditorium still faced each other across the
fountain in Civic Square. Except for the increase in pedestrian
malls and pocket parks, the downtown area had not changed
greatly. The most noticeable differences were the absence of
litter, noise, and exhaust fumes that had overwhelmed my city
back in 1975. The few vehicles that passed me on the surface
streets were practically noiseless.

You can observe a lot just by watching.
—YOGI BERRA

The city had the fresh scent of a spring day in the country
from the profusion of evergreen and deciduous trees and
shrubs that lined the malls; a cheerful and vigorous reminder
of Excelsior City's wilderness heritage. The expressions on the

faces of the people in this clean and peaceful environment were in vivid contrast to the harassed and anxious people rushing about in the noise and stench of downtown Excelsior City in 1975.

> I have been over into the future, and it works.
> —LINCOLN STEFFENS

I rode in a people pod (a small, capsule-like vehicle that traveled silently on a single track) to the Power Building on the Excelsior College campus. There I was welcomed by Professor Sol Ayre, who escorted me to his laboratory in one corner of the converter control room. A tall, handsome, robust man, he appeared to be in his late sixties. Although his greeting was cordial, he gave the impression of being slightly weary, in the manner of a professor who has explained the same concept over and over to a succession of classes.

> Some people are likable in spite of their unswerving integrity.
> —DON MARQUIS

I was elated to be in the presence of this renowned authority on the generation of power and the inventor of so many solar energy devices.*

I began by explaining that the purpose of my mission was to compile a brief composite history of the changes that had taken place during the past fifteen years. Sol Ayre began by

---

* Author's Note: Obviously these devices remain to be perfected by some latter-day Edison. While Sol Ayre and his devices are fictional, similar inventions are today no longer in the science-fiction class. Most of them could be built today. I should like to add, further, that 1990 is obviously not the 1984 of George Orwell. Neither is it the Cloud-Cuckoo-Town of Aristophanes' comedy, the mystical sanctuary of James Hilton's Shangri-La, the behavioristic Walden II of B. F. Skinner, nor the Utopia of Thomas More. What it is, is a commonsense, down-to-earth culture that can be achieved by a civilization capable of landing a man on the moon.

> The message from the moon is that no problem need any longer be considered insoluble.
> —NORMAN COUSINS

I was elated to be in the presence of this renowned authority.

describing his early realization that we were headed for shortages of fossil fuels and his interest in the development of alternate sources of power. As he spoke, his somewhat bored
expression dropped away and he became animated and force-
ful. I knew I was in the presence of genius.

> Talent is what you possess; genius is what pos-
> sesses you.
>
> —MALCOLM COWLEY

In sharing with me the ideas that had shaped his life work,
Sol Ayre avoided the specious misuse of analogy. He said we
were like a family living off the food stored in its basement
with no means of replenishment. In economic terms. we were
eating up our capital rather than living on the interest. He described the planet as our capital and the sun as providing our
limitless energy income. The sun delivers 1½ million trillion
horsepower-hours of energy to our planet every year. Only a

tiny fraction of this energy, 1 percent, is converted by green plants into all the food, timber, and other vegetation on earth. Only a tiny fraction of this growth became, eventually, in millions of years, the fossil fuels we were using up so recklessly— natural resources that were potentially much more valuable to mankind for production of petrochemicals. Years ago Sol Ayre realized that we would have to develop heating systems, blast furnaces, transportation, and electrical generator plants run directly by solar radiation.

> The glorious Lamp of Heaven, the Sun.
> —ROBERT HERRICK

Back in his student days Sol had experimented with solar energy, and built and demonstrated his first practical solar heaters.

Sol had been able to continue his development of solar power during his early career as a professor of engineering. As long as he and his graduate students engaged in experi-

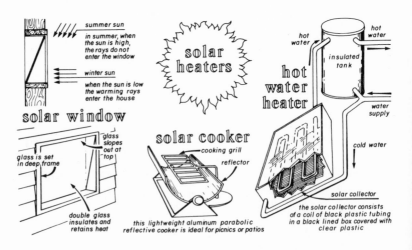

Sol Ayre's first practical solar heaters.

mentation with model solar devices, he experienced little opposition. As a matter of fact, Gene E. All, president of Excelsior College, and Vice-President Grant Swinger were proud to have Sol on the faculty. When conducting tours of the College they invariably included a visit to Sol Ayre's lab to show that token creative work was being done, thereby justifying appeals for increased appropriations.

> Genius is, as a rule, a response to apparently hostile limitations.
>
> —ROBERT LYND

By the late 1950s Sol tried to interest a number of companies in the commercial possibilities of manufacturing his solar equipment but found them unresponsive to his ideas. He then applied for government funding to support the development of a commercial prototype of his solar generator but was turned down by General Overkill, head of the Atmospheric Energy Commission. Of course, the General knew, and so did everyone else, the government was committed to support of the petroleum industry and the development of atomic weapons and energy.

> Lobbyists are the touts of protected industries.
>
> —WINSTON CHURCHILL

A ray of hope appeared when Major E. Clips (Ret.), an influential college trustee, became interested in Sol's work and encouraged him to draft a second proposal for government funding. Sol's hopes were deflated when the Major returned from Washington with the news that Sol could get a substantial grant provided he would redirect his research to the development of solar weaponry in which field, it was said, we were dangerously behind the Russians.

> Adversity is the trial of principle. Without it a man hardly knows whether he is honest or not.
>
> —HENRY FIELDING

However, despite these setbacks, Sol continued his work on domestic solar energy. Then, during the winter of 1963, electrical shortages, brownouts, and blackouts alerted concerned citizens to the possibility of more serious disasters in the future. Sam Mariton, an architect who was stimulated by the challenge of solving problems, sought Sol's help in designing buildings that would generate their own power needs directly from the sun.

> Adversity reveals genius; prosperity conceals it.
> —HORACE

Together Sol and Sam designed some trial buildings able to get their energy free from a solar generator 93 million miles away. The SUNBEAM HOUSE was the first to be designed for solar energy. A solar collector was located on the roof facing south. Additional heat was reflected onto it from the roof of the patio. The collector operated on the same principle as that of a greenhouse. The sun's shortwave rays passed through the clear plastic cover and were converted into longer heat waves, and because these longer waves did not penetrate the clear plastic, the heat was retained. It is more or less what happens when your car heats up inside when you leave it in the sun with the windows closed.

> Everything should be made as simple as possible,
> but not simpler.
> —ALBERT EINSTEIN

Water from an insulated tank below the house was circulated and recirculated through the roof collector so that the water became extremely hot and was then circulated through themostatically controlled baseboard radiators in the house as heat was required. The SUNRAY ALTERED HOUSE, an older dwelling, was modified by adding a solar collector to heat both house and swimming pool. The SOLAR HIGH-RISE COMPLEX consisted of a group of buildings each of which was heated by a convex southern exterior wall consisting of solar cells (photovoltic cells that convert the sun's rays directly into electric energy).

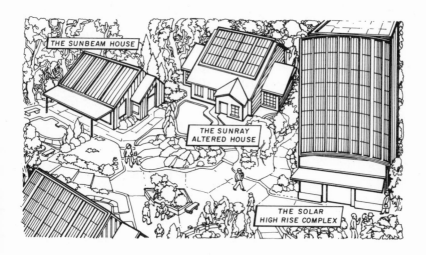

Solar buildings.

After Sol Ayre had demonstrated the practicality of his solar collectors, most designers and builders, with characteristic human resistance to change, ignored his recommendations and dubbed his collectors "Sol's Folly." The new Architecture Building on the Excelsior campus boasted an air-conditioning system that operated uniformly throughout. As a result the occupants of the offices and lecture rooms on the east side of the building suffered in the sweltering heat of the morning sun; those on the west side shivered in the refrigerated air blown into their rooms. The reversal of this situation in the afternoon provided little solace to the victims.

> It is not true that suffering ennobles the character;
> happiness does that sometimes, but suffering, for

the most part, makes men petty and vindictive.
—W. S. Maugham

The new, all-glass Civic Administration Building made do with a popular air-conditioning system that heated the building with a huge furnace and then regulated the temperature by introducing refrigerated air to reduce the heat in order to achieve a comfortable temperature. Sol Ayre was particularly vehement in his condemnation of this system for doubling the waste of energy derived from fossil fuels. Sol discovered that he had accepted the difficult task of trying to sneak the morning sun past the twin roosters of custom and tradition.

Tradition does not mean that the living are dead,
but that the dead are living.
—G. K. Chesterton

Sol was equally annoyed by the lack of adequate insulation in many of the new buildings. The consistent reason for rejecting his recommendations, given by the guardians of the status quo, was the cost factor, even when it was pointed out that over a period of a few years each of the suggested improvements would have paid for themselves.

Consistency requires you to be as ignorant today
as you were a year ago.
—Bernard Berenson

Professor Ayre insisted on providing me with an historical background of the problem that had become generally apparent by 1974. The problem, he said, began back in 1859, when Edwin L. Drake set up the nation's first oil derrick and struck oil on a farm near Titusville, Pennsylvania. From then on, a steady stream of oil led us down the primrose path of industrialization. Oil became synonymous with money and power. From the beginning America led the world in petroleum consumption. As our need for energy grew, giant firms bought control in the facilities of the oil-producing countries. The

United States became the world's greatest squanderer of natural resources. With but 6 percent of the world's population we devoured 33 percent of its energy. In a few years the United States had moved from being one of the energy-rich nations to being one of the most dependent. When the oil-exporting countries decided to throw their weight around and slapped a temporary embargo on crude oil, our petroleum industry declared an energy crisis and used it as an excuse to increase profits.

Excelsior City had been having its own problems with petroleum. In 1972, conservationist groups started action against oil spills in Excelsior Channel. They pressured Mayor C. Nyle and the city council into holding up offshore drilling permits to Beachslic Oil Company until a scientific study of the seabed could be made by competent geologists. Apparently Beachslic Oil had been drilling where there were known faults and fissures but without standby equipment ready to handle any resulting oil spills. When the people saw the oil-soaked birds, fish, and sea animals suffering and dying, a public uproar ensued.

Jeremiah Beachslic, adept at making whole lies out of half-truths, countered with a high-powered, "We'd-like-you-to-know" public relations campaign. He sponsored television commercials showing that there were more birds along the Excelsior coast *after* the Beachslic oil spill. (His commercials neglected to explain that the spill had occurred in midwinter while the commercial was made during the spring migration, when there were always more birds.)

> Advertising is the rattling of a stick inside a swill bucket.
>
> —GEORGE ORWELL

A commercial referring to Beachslic Oil as "The Ecology Company," showed beautiful tropical fish swimming around the pilings of an offshore oil rig. The greatest public relations

The 1974 energy crisis.

Beachslic had no equipment to handle oil spills.

triumph was reserved for a newspaper ad showing Jeremiah Beachslic, the conservationist, planting a tree.

> The purpose of public relations in its best sense is to inform and keep minds open; the purpose of propaganda in the bad sense is to misinform and to keep minds closed.
>
> —JOHN W. HILL

During the 1974 fuel crisis, Beachslic was one of the loudest spokesmen for the petroleum industry. He blamed conservationists for the shortages and demanded unrestricted drilling rights. The industry won everything it asked for: reduction of clean-air standards, increased gasoline and heating oil prices, offshore drilling, and the go-ahead for the environmentally hazardous Alaska Pipeline.

But a flashback to the early settlers of Excelsior Valley shows these pioneers to be men and women who valued their freedom and independence. They made their homes in the valley and farmed the land that sloped down to the river.

But not for long. Lumber companies began their inroads by buying up timber rights to huge tracts of land further upriver and hired the farmers' sons to cut down the trees and haul them away. Sol Ayre's was a voice crying in the wilderness— or what was left of it.

"Over the years," he said, "we were betrayed countless times. *We were betrayed* by the timber baron who promised our young men employment, but when the trees were gone the companies moved on to greener forests. *We were betrayed* by the government, which homesteaded land to early settlers but kept the mineral rights. *We were betrayed* by politicians who conspired with the big, absentee-owned industries that took the rich harvest of trees and the treasures from beneath the soil. The compensation paid the settlers was pitifully small. There was no taxation of the coal companies for hospitals, schools, and other services we should have had. *We were be-*

Jeremiah Beachslic plants a tree.

Beachslic changes his tune.

They made their homes in the valley.

trayed by the schools, which taught that this was industrial progress for Excelsior County. *We were betrayed* as our sons left the farm for the glitter of the city, and the energy industries stripped our valley of its riches of coal, gas, and oil. *We were betrayed* by an education system that taught that this was progress. *We were betrayed* in the city as the welfare system eroded our people's independence while robbing them of their dignity!"

In Excelsior Valley the D. Zaster Mining Company provided employment for awhile, but ruined the area with rapacious strip mining practices. A land of plenty became a bleak region of eroded slopes and polluted streams. Residents who didn't move to the city eventually became habitual welfare recipients.

> Our schools teach the morality of feudalism corrupted by commercialism, and hold up the military

conqueror, the robber baron, and the profiteer, as
models of the illustrious and successful.

—G. B. SHAW

In the D. Zaster operation, bulldozers stripped the topsoil
from the coal seams. Power shovels gouged up the exposed
coal. Tons of vegetation, topsoil, earth, and rock were dumped
downhill or hurled over cliffs in an orgy of ruin.

The silt washed down the slopes and filled the streams.
Rains hurled the waters along, inundating the towns and farmland along the lowland and delta. The sulfur from the coal-
bearing formations produced a solution of sulphuric acid that
polluted the land.

There were mounds of slag containing unrecovered coal
particles along with discharge from the coal-washing operation. Sometimes these ignited and became a burning, simmer-
ing, spewing heap for months at a time. When the rains came,
these piles of waste eroded and oozed down the valley destroying the land and eventually the river. Everything Excelsior
Valley had promised the early settlers was gone. The richness
of coal had left the slag heaps of poverty.

In 1975, the Excelsior Valley Reclamation Authority began
a project to restore the strip-mined areas and to prevent further erosion. The land was reshaped into terraces that followed
the contours of what was left of the structure of the original
valley. These terraces were covered with sanitary landfill and
layers of organic waste. Each new terrace was planted with
deep-rooted grass and converted into grazing pasture for
cattle.

We have to find a better way to develop
and use the riches of this earth.

—OSCAR L. CHAPMAN

Sol Ayre had developed a prototype of a solar farm for the
D. Zaster site but again his proposals met with considerable
resistance.

Logging and strip mining had left a wasteland.

The blighted area was converted into a green pasture.

> When a true genius appears in the world you may
> know him by this sign, that the dunces are all in
> confederacy against him.
> —J. SWIFT

Professor D. Kaye, senior economics adviser, claimed the system was financially unfeasible and accused Sol of being an impractical conservationist and starry-eyed idealist who was willing to upset the American Free Enterprise System in order to save a few unprofitable wildflowers.

> Some men see things as they are and say why. I
> dream things that never were and say, why not?
> —ROBERT F. KENNEDY

Mayor C. Nyle laughed off the Sol Ayre Solar-Saline System as pure science fiction. Jeremiah Beachslic predicted that public funding of solar energy would cause widespread unemployment in the petroleum industry.

Said Beachslic: "The energy companies stand ready to engage in solar energy research if we are given exclusive, long-term rights to the sun, adequate federal subsidies and development money, government backing of our investment, and a twenty-seven percent radiation depletion allowance."

Although the opposition to Sol's proposal was powerful, the 1974 energy crunch generated sufficient concern among the citizenry that reform was possible. Sol and his students by this time had built a demonstration model of the Solar-Saline System.

> Excellence means when a man or woman asks of
> himself more than others do.
> —ORTEGA Y GASSET

When visitors came to see his model, Sol Ayre explained that the Solar-Saline System was an example of the new technology operating in harmony with our environment without pollution and without depleting our natural resources. The system was

Many citizens visited the demonstration model.

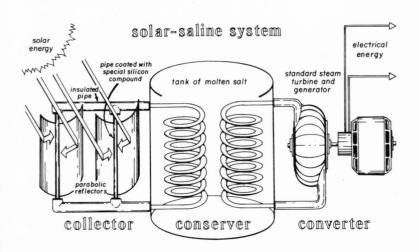

Diagram of the Sol Ayre Solar-Saline System.

ideal for any location with abundant sunlight and this included anywhere between 43° north to 43° south of the equator. (In the Western Hemisphere this would extend from Eugene, Oregon, to Puerto Deseado, Argentina, an area that included nearly all of the United States and South America.)

The diagram delineated by Professor Ayre shows the three major components—the collector, conserver, and converter. The collector, a series of curved reflectors, focuses the sun's rays onto a tiny area occupied by a pipe running the length of the reflector. This collector is based on the same principle as that which a magnifying glass uses to set fire to a piece of paper, and which, according to legend, was employed by Archimedes to set the enemy ships on fire. The unique feature is the pipe's special coating that absorbs heat while also insulating the pipe. Gaseous nitrogen flows through these pipes at a temperature of approximately 1000° F.

The conserver consists of a large, insulated tank of molten salt, which is capable of reaching very high temperatures. The nitrogen at 1000° F passes through a coil inside the tank, transferring its heat to the salt. In a full-size installation the tank of molten salt is capable of storing heat for nighttime use and for days without sunlight.

The converter consists of a second set of coils to absorb the heat and produce steam to drive a conventional turbine and generator.

> I start where the last man left off.
> —THOMAS A. EDISON

Although sunlight is plentiful over most of the earth's surface, it is widely dispersed, so it requires large collection areas. Although the reclaimed D. Zaster site proved unsuitable for many purposes, it was ideally suited for pasture, for growing crops in need of partial shade, and for solar energy collection. The initial one-square-mile solar farm provides more energy than the coal formerly underneath it, in addition to providing power indefinitely.

> Nature, to be commanded, must be obeyed.
> —FRANCIS BACON

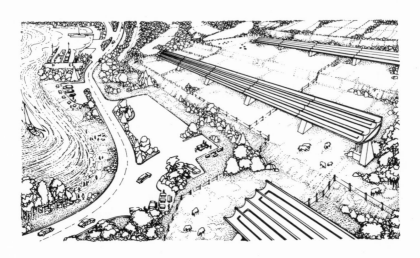

The Sol Ayre Solar Farm.

In the past, citizens of Excelsior City had taken pride in their clean, all-electric homes without realizing that most electricity had been clean only at the consumers' end of the wire. With the availability of abundant, solar-generated power there emerged a heightened interest in ways to use this power to replace the dwindling supply of pollution—producing fossil fuels. Sol Ayre was particularly enthusiastic about the production of two nonpolluting automobiles: (1) The Cy Lance Battery-Powered Car, an ideal little city runabout for one or two people. (Its roof consists of solar cells that keep the battery charged. When there is no sun, it is plugged into a regular electric outlet overnight and will run 150 miles before recharging, but when driven or parked in sunlight recharging is continuous.) (2) The Sue Blyme Hydrogen Car, a vehicle capable of traveling any distance using hydrogen in an internal combustion engine. (Sue Blyme perfected a system to handle liquid hydrogen so that it was considerably safer than gasoline. Solar energy can produce any required amount of hydrogen through electrolysis of water. The burning of hydrogen produces water vapor as its only emission, so that the Sue Blyme system uses only solar energy and water, and releases the water back into the environment.)

Although Sol Ayre's specialty was solar power, he became keenly interested in all nonpolluting power sources. He described dams with underwater generators located in bays where large tidal flows produced abundant power. Generators are installed in breakwaters to harness the power of ocean waves. Turbines are anchored in the deep and powerful ocean currents that move continuously with irresistible force. Even the temperature differences in the ocean are being used. The warm surface water vaporizes and expands ammonia to drive a generator and then the frigid water from the depths condenses the ammonia so that the process is continuous. Windmills at suitable land and sea locations harnessed the power of moving air, which is as free as sunlight. And geothermal power from heat beneath the surface of the earth is also available in abundance and is being widely used. These continuous sources could provide all the electrical power we will ever need. If we should ever need to, we could get still more by sending solar collectors into orbit around the earth.

The Solar-Saline System was developed to meet local needs and therefore required a heat conserver to provide electrical energy for nighttime and peak loads. Heat conservers would be practically unnecessary in solving the country's energy problems through the establishment of a national grid. A national grid would tie the major sources of power production and consumption together to distribute local surpluses to wherever

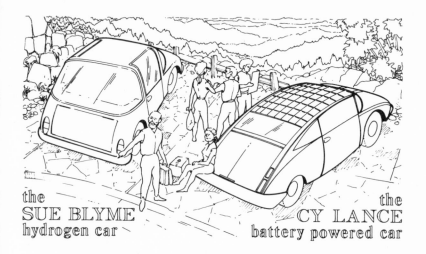

Sol Ayre was enthusiastic about the Sue Blyme and Cy Lance cars.

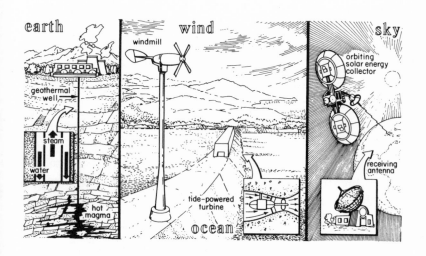

There are many nonpolluting power sources.

needed. We already have some effective regional grids, but the national system resembles a confusion of interstate highways, gravel roads, cow paths, foot trails, detours, and unbuilt bridges.

> Without a good systems analysis and systems design as a first step, or at least as a parallel effort, it is not easy to describe, understand, and specify the pieces of the solution.
>
> —SIMON RAMO

If three electrical systems are connected and one loses its generating capacity, chances are the combined system will have a brownout. But if all systems are interconnected they can take care of any emergency. A coast-to-coast grid would take advantage of the differences in time. Peak usage in the evening in New York would draw on our daylight surplus here on the West Coast.

> Light is the task when many share the toil.
>
> —HOMER

If international cooperation continues to grow, we can look forward to the day when we will have a world grid. This would make continuous energy abundant and available everywhere, because as the world turns half the world is always in sunlight when the other half is in darkness.

> My country is the world. My countrymen are all mankind.
>
> —WILLIAM LLOYD GARRISON

My interview was over. The hour was late. I was physically tired, but mentally exhilarated by the exciting concepts so clearly set forth.

> The great creative individual is capable of more wisdom and virtue than collective man ever can be.
>
> —JOHN STUART MILL

CHAPTER V

People

City living, under safe conditions, has a pulse and
an excitement that rural living cannot match. It
would seem likely that in the years ahead some of
the most appealing residential areas in America
would be found in such rehabilitated urban en-
claves.

—JAMES A. MICHENER

I KNEW that Excelsior City's ex-mayor, Harold Foresight, was
considered to be the mobilizing force behind the developments
that had taken place during his three terms in office. I was
curious to know how he had managed to pull the many diverse
elements together to create this new and beautiful city. After
meeting him I had part of the answer. Foresight is an impressive, intelligent man who communicates his wide-ranging
knowledge with precision and in the language of the people
who he served. I interviewed him in his home. His office-den
is a large, nondescript room cluttered with piles of papers and
hundreds of books on philosophy, city planning, management,
and a wide range of related subjects.

I found Foresight to be not only amazingly well informed
but also a warm, engaging, occasionally witty man. He had
obviously enjoyed being mayor as much as he enjoyed now
being adviser to a number of civic organizations and chairman
of the planning commission.

Foresight described the city and its people.

> If you want to get across an idea, wrap it up in a
> person.
>   —RALPH BUNCHE

Foresight did not dwell for long on the problems of civic
government prior to his administration, but he had little to say
in favor of his predecessors. He appeared to take a certain delight in ridiculing ex-Mayor C. Nyle's favorite quote: "I have
seen the past and it works" by rephrasing it "I have seen the
past and it's worse." He admitted that 1975 was a bad year
for the cities everywhere, but felt that Mayor C. Nyle's administration had established a new low in status quo government.

> When we got into office, the thing that surprised
> me most was to find that things were just as bad as
> we'd been saying they were.
>   —J. F. KENNEDY

Nyle's advisers all had vested interests in maintaining business as usual. The president of the council, Barry Cade, was an obstructionist who could be relied upon, in any suggested change of policy, to produce the improbable, hypothetical situation in which the new policy could not work.

> He'll doublecross that bridge when he comes to it.
> —OSCAR LEVANT

Phil A. Buster, chairman of the planning commission, did little more than broadcast inept speeches over radio and television about the importance of planning.

> Every improvement in communication makes the
> bore more terrible.
> —FRANK MOORE COLBY

Phil A. Buster's speechmaking had the approval of the planning commission since it provided a cover for activities of the commission members, three women real estate dealers— Laurel Canyon, Beverly Hills, and Belle Aire—and two land developers, J. P. Getall and Cess Pool.

> Since we have to speak well of the dead, let's knock
> them while they're alive.
> —JOHN SLOAN

Jerry Bilt, who maintained under-the-table connections with real estate promoters and housing contractors, was chairman of the housing commission, the members of which were slumlords Pearl Loin and Rob Berry, along with Monty Banks and Will Sindell, two chicanerous lawyers specializing in land development deals.

> Examples I could cite you more;
> But be content with these four;
> For when one's proofs are aptly chosen
> Four are as valid as four dozen.
> —MATTHEW PRIOR

Foresight felt that a number of factors contributed to his

landslide victory over the entrenched political establishment with its solid financial support. Ed Itor of the *Excelsior Daily Log* had exposed some of the pay-off rackets at City Hall. A general disenchantment with the crowded, smoggy, noisy, crime-ridden city and a growing desire for peace, quiet, and the simple pleasures, contributed to the success of Foresight's campaign for a cleaner, safer city. C. Nyle and his group had nothing to offer but the same tired old slogans.

> Anybody can win, unless there happens to be a second entry.
>
> —GEORGE ADE

Harold Foresight's political philosophy was based on the concept that in spite of political, racial, or religious differences, all humans are subject to the laws of nature in the same way as are all other living things. As a political independent he rejected party politics that polarized issues. He claimed that political extremes of either the Right or Left only determined which kind of political leadership would lead us to our doom. He maintained this independence because no political party had offered a logical program for utilizing science and technology to achieve harmony with natural laws, to preserve our environment, and to assure us of a future. Without implementation of our knowledge and the ability to assess our lives and restructure our behavior for survival, our most advanced civilization was in danger of being the shortest-lived civilization.

> An independent is a person who wants to take the politics out of politics.
>
> —ADLAI STEVENSON

One of the shortest paths to doom is to use stopgap, piecemeal measures in our quest for survival. Foresight's political predecessors had dealt with each crisis as it arose. For every problem they solved, a bigger one was created.

> Reality has limits: stupidity has not.
> —NAPOLEON BONAPARTE

Foresight explained the economic problems facing Excelsior City, the country, and the world back in 1975. During the early 1970s the wealthy industrial nations were complacent about the economy and trusted the modern mythology of unlimited growth and affluence. Suddenly people the world over were conscious of runaway inflation, coupled with an economically incongruous recession, industrial breakdowns, strikes, shortages, excessive profits, a wildly fluctuating stock market, and growing unemployment. In America, the president's panicky advisers dealt with the problem as though a modicum of adjustments in the monetary system would put things to right.

> If ignorance paid dividends most Americans could make a fortune out of what they don't know about economics.
> —LUTHER HODGES

The typical response of each government agency was a rush to its own defense by tightening the enforcement of its self-serving regulations, thus assuring its own perpetuation rather than helping solve the country's dilemma. Meanwhile big business pushed ahead in its same old exploitive direction, so that together government and business fostered a stultifying bureaucratic establishment that made the crisis inevitable.

> Things fall apart; the center cannot hold;
> Mere anarchy is loosed upon the world,
> The blood-dimmed tide is loosed and everywhere
> The ceremony of innocence is drowned;
> The best lack all conviction while the worst
> Are full of passionate intensity.
> —WILLIAM BUTLER YEATS

Professor D. Kaye described the recession of 1975 as a recurrence of the crash of 1929 and the Great Depression of the 1930s. Unfortunately many economists accepted this simplistic concept and viewed the problem as simply a monetary crisis. *The economists did not understand that what was*

happening in 1975 was not a monetary crisis, but technologi-
cal society escalated to its level of incompetence.

> Practical men who believe themselves exempt from
> any intellectual influences, are usually the slaves of
> some defunct economist.
>   —JOHN MAYNARD KEYNES

The Great Depression was a breakdown of the country's
monetary system. The late 1920s were a time of abundance.
Oil wells gushed forth more petroleum than could be consumed. Granaries were bursting and milk and meat were
plentiful. Energy, food, and all manner of consumer products
were in oversupply while available jobs were in undersupply.
The monetary crisis of the Depression era, widespread poverty,
and overproduction of goods could have been solved by
placing more purchasing power into the hands of the people
and thereby increasing the demand for products.

> One of the strangest things about life is that the
> poor who need money the most, are the very ones
> that never have it.
>   —FINLEY PETER DUNNE

The so-called "monetary crisis" of 1975 could not be controlled by the traditional economic stabilizers. Inflation, recession, and unemployment were symptoms of an ecological
crisis consisting of a population explosion, a deteriorating environment, and a shortage of food, energy, and other resources. Although temporary shortages of beef, grain, steel,
and building materials along with spiraling prices had been
evident for some time, the energy crisis caused greater widespread disruption of society. Because we had failed to develop
a diversified energy base we were overly dependent upon fossil
fuels. In the beginning this was cheap energy. Coal was readily
available and relatively shallow wells provided a bonanza of
oil. In other words, the energy required to mine for coal or
drill for oil was very small in relation to the abundant return
of energy. As the most accessible sources were depleted it took

more energy to get energy. More of the earth's surface had to be destroyed to get at the coal. More feet of well had to be drilled to get at the oil. The only government-sponsored alternate source was atomic energy. This turned out to be the most expensive of all. It took more energy to develop atomic energy than it did to exploit fossil fuels. Breakdowns, shutdowns, and near catastrophies had reduced the output of atomic power plants to the point that they demanded great input and produced little output.

> What is wanted is not the will to believe but the
> wish to find out, which is the exact opposite.
>   —BERTRAND RUSSELL

Energy shortages, inflation of the cost of energy, and unemployment were inevitable even if an energy crisis had not been precipitated by the oil sheikhs. The 1975 recession, inflation, and unemployment were the result of depletion of environmental resources rather than of surpluses.

> The crisis stems not from a deficiency of demand
> but of supply, the most dramatic manifestations of
> which have been shortages of food and soaring
> food prices, and shortages of oil and soaring energy
> prices.
>   —LEONARD SILK

At the national level, the President initiated one phase of his economic recovery plan after another. Each phase was intended to correct the havoc caused by the last but only compounded it.

> The Nixon Political Principle: If two wrongs don't
> make a right—try three.

The failure of the economy to respond positively to subsidies, tax incentives, quotas, and price and wage controls resulted in the President resorting to the Pentagon Panacea: boosting the economy by increasing the military budget to create pro tem employment.

> The Ford Employment Principle: If everybody
> was in the army there'd be no unemployment.

Unfortunately the low ratio of employees to cost in the munitions industries resulted in billions being spent on military hardware and vast quantities of natural resources being devoted to destructive or nonproductive purposes while little impact was made on unemployment. The next Presidential move was to blame the public for inflation and urge the populace to practice restraint and purchase only bare essentials. Increased recession and unemployment followed. The next Presidential approach was to cut taxes to stimulate the economy.

> The Ford Economic Principle: Bite the bullet and
> save your pennies and I'll lower your taxes so
> you'll have more money not to spend.

The energy shortage became the next issue for Presidential attention, so he proposed to increase the gasoline tax in order to inflate the price of fuel so that people would buy less. To offset the effect of this on the economy he released billions of dollars for highway construction.

> The Ford Energy Principle: I will reduce the consumption of gasoline and build more highways for
> you not to drive on.

The real wealth of the planet is its natural resources. Our real wealth is our ability to use these resources without destroying their source. Money has no value unless it represents energy, food, materials, or products. No amount of monetary manipulation can create natural resources.

> I'm scared! I don't know whether the world is full
> of smart men bluffing . . . or imbeciles who
> mean it.
>
> —MORRIE BRICKMAN

Every attempt to reduce controls on environmental quality

as a trade-off for resolving the economic crisis deepens rather than resolves the crisis. The only possible lasting solution is to base our monetary system on a sound ecological system. Economic problems can no longer be solved by a flow of cheap raw materials from the poor countries to the rich. Lasting solutions to economic and energy problems are provided by ecologically sound developments such as the Sol Ayre Solar Farm.

> Now there is one outstandingly important fact regarding Spaceship Earth, and that is that no instruction book came with it.
> —R. BUCKMINSTER FULLER

The real challenge that confronted us in 1975 was not only to stabilize the economy but to find a way to use our monetary system to resolve the ecological crisis and shift the monetary system to a realistic environmental base. The obstacles to this were formidable because the military-industrial complex and other big-money powers were the greatest environmental destroyers.

> There is fast forming in this country an aristocracy of wealth, the worst form of aristocracy that can curse the prosperity of a nation.
> —PETER COOPER

Harold Foresight had finished his discourse on his political and economic philosophy and now turned to the application of these concepts in the reconstruction of Excelsior City.

> Ideas shape the course of history.
> —JOHN MAYNARD KEYNES

By 1975, the inner-city had deteriorated deplorably. The middle class and the wealthy had deserted it for suburbia. The business district was abandoned at night. The old areas of town houses and apartments had become slums and businesses had begun moving to the suburbs. Instead of trying the old strategy of strengthening the central business core, Foresight decided to revitalize the city beginning at the center by creating buildings that were beautiful and attractive to live in, buildings that would promote social involvement, ease of living, and safety. His aim was to make Excelsior Center a twenty-four-hour-a-day community. In 1975, downtown Excelsior City was a nine-to-five operation.

Recycling commerical buildings into diversified structures began with the thirty-story Excelsior Commercial Building. The first three floors became a shopping center. The next twelve floors were retained as commercial offices and the top fifteen floors were converted into attractive, comfortable, reasonably priced apartments. The shopping center was active at night, and there was a feeling of life in the building at all times.

> Not life, but a good life, is to be chiefly valued.
> —SOCRATES

Many who moved into the beautiful Renaissance Towers at the top of the Commercial Building were people who worked in the downtown offices and shopping center. The first to make the move were mature citizens whose children were grown. They were willing to give up the morning and evening traffic battle and travel by elevator to work, exchanging a long horizontal for a short vertical trip. They had literally hours of extra free time every week. They could spend it quietly or they could attend live theater, visit art galleries and museums—take advantage of all the things an active city can offer.

> To be able to fill leisure intelligently is the last
> product of civilization.
> —ARNOLD TOYNBEE

The Renaissance Tower concept spread to the suburbs. The Excelsior Park Plaza had been a luxury suburban apartment

*Each morning thousands joined the crush of traffic
headed for the city.*

At day's end they joined the exodus from the city.

complex that was now converted into Renaissance Buildings, with shopping, business, light industry, and services such as medical and health care, arts and crafts studios, and educational facilities, all in the same park-like surroundings that people had moved there for in the first place. Many quit their city jobs and transferred to jobs in their own buildings.

Now more individuals can choose to work and play in the city center or in the suburbs without spending hours in hazardous commuting. People are happier. Air is cleaner. Energy savings are enormous, and the need for highways and public transportation is reduced. Essentially, more people are working at home.

> Home was quite a place when people stayed there.
> —E. B. WHITE

As the older sections were rebuilt with attractively landscaped Renaissance Buildings Excelsior Center became more secure and many who had left the city returned, because city life enjoys a pulse and an excitement that suburban living lacks.

> Tower'd cities please us then,
> And the busy hum of men.
> —JOHN MILTON

The Excelsior Center plan was financed by taxation principles derived from the social sciences. The property-tax base was changed from a material value to a societal value system. Old city structures like the Excelsior Commercial Building had placed heavy demands on the city in terms of both public and private transportation, resulting in the use of excessive energy and a great waste of human time and effort. The societal tax assessment of the Excelsior Commercial Building was increased to compensate for the money and human energy it consumed. When the plans for the Renaissance Towers were submitted, the owners of the Excelsior Commercial Building were assured that after the recycling and renovating of the building the tax would be based on only a fraction of its previous assessment. The new method of basing assessments on societal value did not force anyone to recycle a building. But those who wanted to retain a property that was a drain on human and material resources knew they would be highly taxed. New structures that were designed as components of the Renaissance Plan paid comparatively low taxes. In this way construction based on societal values was rewarded.

> Reinforcing a response produces an increase in the probability that the response will occur again.
> —B. F. SKINNER

The societal principle was eventually applied to all taxation. Automobile licenses included a low minimum, plus increments based on the vehicle's pollutant emissions. This encouraged owners of petroleum-powered cars to have their smog control devices in good working order at the required inspection for annual licensing and encouraged early replacement of petroleum-powered vehicles with the newer non-polluting vehicles.

> The perpetual obstacle to human advancement is custom.
> —JOHN STUART MILL

Back in 1975, most transportation experts recommended public rapid transit oriented to making it easier for city people to move to the suburbs. This accelerated the demise of the city. The Excelsior City priorities were (1) stop the escalation of unnecessary transportation; (2) make it easy for the city dweller to get from one part of the city to another safely and comfortably; and (3), provide a mass-transit system for those who still had to commute. If the commuter service had been built first these objectives could not have been achieved.

In the City Center pedestrian malls, lanes for owner-

*This could not have been achieved if commuter service
had been built first.*

operated cars and for bicycles and other people-powered vehicles are on the surface level. The tracks for people pods
are built into the sides of the second story of the buildings
so one can ride from one building to another or one part of
the city to another. Those who prefer to walk can take a sky-
walk at the third-story level.

All the commuter trains from the suburbs and outlying
villages become subways as they enter Excelsior City. No
matter what the outside temperature or climatic conditions
people can stroll through several miles of attractive prome-
nades where the temperature never varies and the air is pure
and fresh. If they have other business to conduct, they can
leave the bright and colorful subterranean city and enter any
of the major buildings at the basement level.

Zoning has provided for a wide variety of life-styles. The
city took over a depressed district of old town houses and
renamed it Excelsior Homesteads. A low-income family that

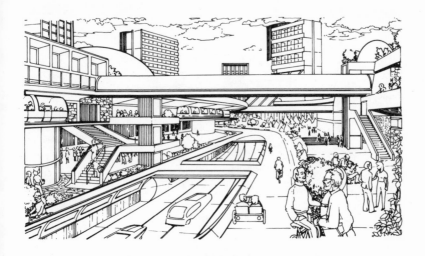

The City Center transportation system.

wanted to homestead was given a house and required to bring
it up to acceptable standards of safety and appearance within
a year. A team of qualified tradespeople was available to help
with repairs, renovation, and advice. A tract of city land was
named Excelsior Wonderland and zoned for creative and in-
novative housing.

> What would the world be without variety?
> Soon all would die of sameness or satiety.
> —J. WALTER WALSH

Back in 1975, the director of welfare, P. Brayne, and his
assistant, Molly Coddle, were social workers of the old school.
They believed that you could give dignity to a person by
giving him a handout. The failure of the P. Brayne theory
to produce human dignity along with the increasing depen-
dence of welfare recipients, resulted in the development of a
new kind of "welfare" system, in which each person could

*Excelsior Wonderland accommodated creative people and
experimental housing.*

discover his or her own dignity by serving society in the way
he or she was best suited. Individuals should not be valued
only for their economic productivity; social productivity is
equally important. Every person not employed in regular, commercial work was given an opportunity for a job in civilian
service. People who used to be on welfare earned bonus payments for their contributions to society. Under a new system,
a former welfare recipient could be paid a bonus for keeping
his or her apartment or house in good condition and earn an
additional bonus for working to keep the neighborhood clean
and safe and attractive.

> Run, if you like, but try to keep your breath;
> Work like a man, but don't be worked to death.
> —O. W. HOLMES

Some elderly persons joined the grandparent program and
spent their hours giving love and care to institutionalized re-

tarded children. Others helped in day-care centers and kinder-gartens bringing a wealth of experience to the young.

> The heads of strong old age are beautiful
> Beyond all grace of youth.
> —ROBINSON JEFFERS

The program has restored personal dignity to those who would otherwise be getting handouts. It has built cleaner, safer neighborhoods. It has helped fulfill the emotional needs of people who used to be neglected and alone.

> Though pride is not a virtue,
> it is the parent of many virtues.
> —J. C. COLLINS

Another quiet revolution took place—a gradual shift to people power for transportation and recreation. People began using the malls and skywalks for recreational walking, since they could walk nearly anywhere in the city without having to cross vehicular traffic. The curb-lane bikeways in Excelsior Center and the bikeways separated from the highways in the suburbs accommodate a variety of people-powered vehicles. The shift to people power has brought people closer to na-ture. The old popular recreational vehicles were motorcycles, dune buggies, snowmobiles, and power boats that produced noise pollution, smell pollution, and ecological havoc. Now the recreational emphasis is on personal fulfillment, through physical activity and a more peaceful, intimate contact with nature.

In concluding his description of fifteen years of progress in Excelsior City, Harold Foresight observed that most construc-tive solutions were the result of integrating concepts from two opposite directions. Some ideas emerged from the grass roots level through involvement of the people closest to the prob-lems. The citizens' proposed solutions were incorporated into the total system being developed by the planners. This inter-

The earth does not belong to man—man belongs to the earth.

action between individual and sometimes fragmentary answers emerging from citizen participation and the rational function of systems dynamics resulted in solutions that were a synthesis accommodating immediate needs while fulfilling the requirements of overall planning. Fortunately, in spite of strong opposition to planning, and the controls implied by planning, sufficient popular support was obtained so that steady improvement of living conditions for the people in Excelsior City was achieved.

> Only within the moment of time represented by the present century has one species—man—acquired significant power to alter the nature of his world.
> —RACHEL CARSON

CHAPTER VI

Progress

This is the first age that's paid much attention to the future, which is a little ironic since we may not have one.

—ARTHUR C. CLARKE

THE office of Marv Ellis, senior systems analyst for Excelsior City, was flooded with light from skylights in the ceiling and windows along the north wall. The room contained several large tables, each with a stack of sketches and charts. After hearing about the monumental achievements of Marv Ellis, I was expecting to meet a much older man than the one who now welcomed me. Although Marv Ellis was fifty-five years old, as I discovered later, he appeared at least ten years younger. He was a compactly built, neatly dressed man with an intense manner. As he spoke, he would turn from time to time to look directly into my eyes, as if searching to be sure that his meaning was being understood. His concern was unnecessary, as I found his discourse to be quite clear and easy to follow.

Marv Ellis began by explaining how he conceptualized Excelsior City as a total system. He described systems dynamics as a process for understanding how things interact one with another and one in which all the elements can be brought into proper relationship to resolve difficult problems. The goal of

I visited Marv Ellis in his office.

systems dynamics was the development of new patterns of interrelationships through which the city's social, civic, and environmental problems could be more easily solved. Although the basis of systems dynamics was logic, common sense had to be augmented by massive quantities of detailed knowledge. The space program had shown how a complex undertaking could be managed. It had shown that billions of dollars, hundreds of thousands of people, thousands of contractors and subcontractors and their many overlapping functions could operate effectively together when systems dynamics were used to control precise methods for keeping track of all the elements. This was the opposite of the traditional crisis-management approach—the Band-Aid approach. By continuing to exploit the potential of every technological development, we unleash vast forces without the capacity to predict long-term consequences. Our survival requires that past preoccupation with the mastery of nature turn into a preoccupation with the mastery of ourselves.

> We live in a Newtonian world of Einsteinian physics ruled by Frankensteinian logic.
> —DAVID RUSSELL

Back in 1970, when the federal government implemented cutbacks affecting the entire aerospace industry—and panic struck the workers in one of Excelsior Ctiy's major industries —Supersonic Zeppelin laid off hundreds of engineers and technicians.

Hans Zup and many of his co-workers threw in the towel and set about finding other jobs before their unemployment benefits expired. But Gustav Wind and the more militant workers initiated a campaign to force the federal government to continue subsidizing Supersonic Zeppelin.

Through effective mobilization of community support, a measure of relief was achieved. First the *Excelsior Daily Log* carried editorials insisting that if subsidies for Supersonic Zeppelin did not continue, the country would lose its leadership position in the world of aviation.

> Man is a reasoning rather than a reasonable animal.
> —ALEXANDER HAMILTON

Jeremiah Beachslic, president of the International Petroleum Producers Association, met with members of the oil lobby. He convinced them of the SSZ's importance to the petroleum industry. He urged them to use every means at their disposal to obtain an extended subsidy of the SSZ program.

> I care not who makes the laws of a nation if I can get out an injunction.
> —FINLEY PETER DUNNE

Excelsior's popular Senator, Gabriel Trumpet, clearly saw the importance of the SSZ program to his constituents. He forthwith introduced a compromise bill that would finance the development of prototypes of the SSZ but would not support production of the airship beyond the research and prototype phase. This interesting bill met nearly everybody's needs. It providently saved face for our President, Mack E. Velly, since it continued the administration's program of developing the SSZ after the Congress had decided that the country did not need it. It also put some of Supersonic Zeppelin's influential and highest-paid executives and engineers back to work. It pleased the superpatriots who felt that their country must lead *all* other countries in *all* areas of human endeavor. It reassured the military-industrial complex that the President would continue to support projects rejected by the people's representatives, "in the interest of national security." And finally, because no actual program of building and flying SSZs was to be undertaken, it temporarily silenced opposition of the ecologically minded citizens who were concerned about pollution, the destruction of the atmosphere's protective ozone layer, and the potential damage from sonic booms. It also defused the arguments of critics who felt that the SSZs would benefit only the very few who would fly in them—and yet be paid for from the pocketbooks of all the taxpayers. The Trumpet Bill was a political triumph, and ensured Senator Trumpet's re-election.

Unfortunately the Trumpet Bill provided only temporary relief for the very pressing problems of Excelsior City. Many competent engineers were still out of work. At Excelsior College, Professor Owen Thinker was heavily pressured to stop his attacks on contributors to environmental degradation. C. Clearly was frustrated in his attempts to obtain approval for a public education program of teaching for survival. The board of the Baron Bank, which included Jeremiah Beachslic, Professor D. Kaye, and Frank N. Stein (president of Super Sonic Zeppelin), could not see its way clear to approve the "wasteful" financing of a project to use the considerable talents

Prototype of the SSZ.

of the unemployed engineers in solving the housing, energy, transportation, and pollution problems of the city. Besides, as the board pointed out, it would be inflationary.

> Banking may be a career from which no man really recovers.
> —JOHN KENNETH GALBRAITH

Professor D. Kaye responded to the city's crisis by organizing the Committee for Expediency in Solving Shortages. The committee ran advertisements in the Excelsior City morning paper, *The Post Picayune Polemic,* blaming inflation and the shortage of oil, building materials, and beef upon the conservationists. It cited the environmentalists' opposition to offshore drilling in Excelsior Channel, their resistance to logging operations in Excelsior Wilderness Park, and their fight against use of carcinogenic growth hormones in beef cattle. The ads were signed by the *Committee Representing All the People:*

D. Kaye, Beachslic; Rob R. Baron; Frank N. Stein; Lum Barr from Clear Cut Logging; and Mal Ignant, from B. Zarr Meats. The committee, subsequently known as CRAP, had banded together to interfere with efforts to find real solutions to our problems.

> My rackets are run on strictly American lines and they're going to stay that way.
> —AL CAPONE

Soon after being elected, Mayor Harold Foresight established the Committee for Social and Environmental Planning and commissioned it to set up a planning and development subcommittee of the unemployed engineers to be known as SAVE (Social Action Voluntary Engineers). Marv Ellis was named chairman. Hume N. Knight, who had replaced P. Brayne as director of social welfare, was vice-chairman. The balance of the committee consisted of Gloria Femme from the Association of Women, Angel Black from the Inner-City Ethnic Union, Phil N. Thropic from the Community Foundation, Steve Adore from United Labor, and Pete Moss from the Ecological Conservation Society, along with a group of engineers—Tex Nology, Mary Torious, Vic Tory, Jean Yuss, Hugh Main, and Al Truism.

These individuals were the best available, all honestly dedicated to solving problems. However, each was a specialist lacking in the comprehensiveness required to implement a systems dynamics scheme. Hume N. Knight, for example, was a social scientist specializing in social welfare for the poor. It took time before he realized that the problems of the poor could not be effectively solved in isolation from the other problems of society, and that the prosperity of all depended on the condition of the physical environment.

> Man's burden is himself.
> —MAURICE FREEHILL

Committee for Social and Environmental Planning, from left to right, Hume N. Knight, Jean Yuss, Pete Moss, Mary Torious, Angel Black, Marv Ellis, Gloria Femme, Tex Nology, Vic Tory, Al Truism, Steve Adore, Hugh Main, unidentified flasher (not a member), and Mimi O'Graff, secretary.

Pete Moss, an environmentalist expert in the complexity of ecosystems, still needed to acquire greater understanding of technology and human behavior.

> Nature is an infinite sphere whose center is everywhere and whose circumference is nowhere.
> —BLAISE PASCAL

Gloria Femme, though working strenuously for women's rights, began to understand through her involvement with the process of systems dynamics that the achievement of equality on a treadmill to oblivion would be a no-win victory.

> Most hierarchies were established by men who now monopolize the upper levels, thus depriving women of their rightful share of opportunities for incompetence.
> —L. J. PETER

Angel Black came to a similar realization. If her efforts helped only blacks and other minorities to gain their share in a city that would eventually turn into a ghost town, no matter how valiant those efforts, they would be like carrying water in a sieve.

> We destroyed slavery but not racism.
> —HENRY STEELE COMMAGER

It was difficult and still is difficult for individuals to comprehend that most problems are interdependent. This does not always mean that all problems can be solved simultaneously but that each individual solution should contribute to the total solution.

> There are no islands any more.
> —EDNA ST. VINCENT MILLAY

Our studies showed that there was no transportation system, that is, no total system that integrated all the various means of travel into a coordinated whole. Of course, there were freighters and ocean liners that docked at the piers in Excelsior Bay. There was a railway system (or, in the case of passenger trains, the remains of one). There was an airport (twenty-eight miles from the city). There was a system of roads, highways, and freeways used by automobiles, trucks, and buses. Each of these systems operated under a different authority, and consequently, each was in competition with the other. None of these constituted a complete transportation system. The railroad station, airport, docks, and bus depot were located many miles apart. Time schedules were not coordinated, and getting from one terminal to another was frequently the most difficult and hazardous part of the trip.

> Commuter—one who spends his life
> In riding to and from his wife:
> A man who shaves and takes a train
> And then rides back to shave again.
> —E. B. WHITE

A first step was to stop the financing of mass transportation until some other problems were solved. Historically, it had been shown that every improvement of mass transportation to and from the city not only had produced a worse tangle downtown, it had also helped to accelerate central-city decay and to expand urban sprawl.

The wrecks of the past were America's warnings.
—GEORGE BANCROFT

Marv Ellis went on to explain that the installation of visionphones in all civic offices had reduced the need for travel. City officials were able to have face-to-face conferences without leaving their offices. Plans, charts, documents, and tables of figures could be shared instantly on the screen of the visionphone. Special visionphone conference rooms were made available in all major buildings so that group meetings could take place without loss of travel time. The visionphone was a boon to the business community. It captured the essence of the reality of being in the same room with persons who might be next door or anyplace in the world. It took only a small fraction of the energy to send the visual and auditory image of a person as it did to transport the person from one place to another. The individual who had not spent time and effort in traveling was much better prepared mentally for rational thought and meaningful communication. In the past, diplomats flew halfway around the world, arriving for vitally important meetings mentally disoriented and with digestive and other bodily functions out of synchronization with their new time schedules.

The redevelopment of Excelsior Center had reduced the need for transportation, but the freeways were still a major problem and were frequently the scene of unofficial demolition derbies. This problem was resolved when the freeways were converted into automated guideways. The automobile enters the guideway by a special access ramp. By simply turning off

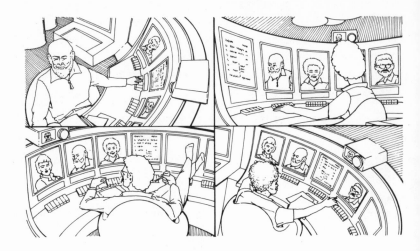

Visionphone conference rooms are available so that group meetings require no travel time.

the hydrogen engine or electric motor and inserting a credit card in a slot in the dashboard, the vehicle is tied into communication, control, and power that then takes over operation of the car. A central computer selects the fastest routing and reserves guideway space all the way to the end of the preselected trip. In seconds the car merges with the hundred-mile-per-hour traffic on the guideway. The passengers can relax as the guideway traffic speeds along. At the exit station the car is routed automatically to a parking area. One eight-foot-wide guideway has the traffic capacity of fifteen of the old twelve-foot traffic lanes.

The system of people pods, which originally served only within Excelsior Center, now provides interconnections with the railroad station, airport, docks, and bus depot, as well as other strategic terminals throughout the city. Each pod seats four people or two people with luggage. One simply enters an empty pod, slips a credit card in the slot, and presses the

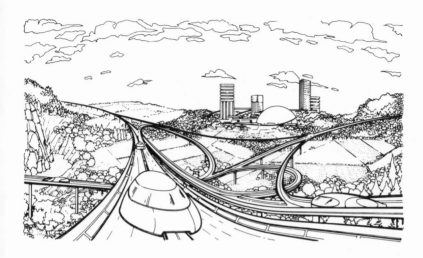

One eight-foot-wide guideway has the traffic capacity of fifteen of the old twelve-foot traffic lanes.

destination button. A computer guides the pod nonstop along the sides of buildings or through them, or through underground tunnels. At its destination it is shunted off the main line, where one only has to get out and walk away.

High-speed trains that can travel at up to 500 miles per hour enter and leave the downtown Excelsior Center Depot. These trains have speed, economy, convenience, comfort, and safety. They are nonpolluting, linear-induction-powered, and aircushioned. They have replaced the airplane for domestic use—for all but a dwindling number of old-time flying buffs.

Marv Ellis used this description of the transportation system to illustrate the systems idea and to show why it was necessary to study transportation needs in relation to individual needs and the total Excelsior City concept before any consideration was given to the specific means of transportation. The only groups that were displeased with the results were car thieves, airplane hijackers, and auto body repairmen.

*The pods move nonstop along the sides of, or through, buildings,
and in underground tunnels.*

*The train has replaced the airplane for all but a dwindling number
of oldtime flying buffs.*

Men are not against you; they are merely for themselves.

—GENE FOWLER

Through systems dynamics consistent progress was made
toward minimizing our destructive impact on the natural environment. We are learning to use all of our resources with
maximum efficiency and effectiveness. We have reversed our
old concepts about material. What used to be called waste, or
scrap, is today our major material resource, and we reserve
our untapped natural resources as our back-up supply. Today,
nearly all products and their component parts are coded either
magnetically, isotopically, or by color, for material content.
When an appliance, container, or other product has fulfilled
its usefulness it is recycled and the coding eliminates the high
cost of material separation. Of course, nature had no need to
separate materials for recycling, but man has changed the
form of some elements, so we must sort them out. We are also
recycling great amounts of organic material for agricultural
fertilizers.

Judgment is not the knowledge of fundamental
laws; it is knowing how to apply a knowledge of
them.

—CHARLES GOW

There is an absence of trash containers in Excelsior Center
because downtown buildings are connected to a vacuum system
that collects all the garbage in about twenty minutes. A central
underground separator extracts and sorts paper, metallic objects, glass, and organic matter. At long last we have learned
to adopt nature's plan of dealing with waste by recycling
everything over and over again. We have not only developed
the mechanical means of recycling, but we have found ways
of enhancing the earth's own recycling systems.

We have cultivated patches of organic soil in the landscaped areas in the Excelsior Center malls, boulevards, and

parks, because we found that organic soil that is rich in micro-organisms will consume vast amounts of carbon monoxide. We have practically eliminated mosquitoes from the area by supplying the wetland areas with hatchery-bred minnows. These little fish eat the mosquito larvae without the environmentally damaging effects of insecticides.

> Nature never breaks her own laws.
> —LEONARDO DA VINCI

We cleaned up the pollution in our lakes by introducing a variety of fish called the white amur. It gobbles up aquatic weed, algae, and garbage, while growing to a length of three feet and a weight of seventy pounds. The white amur does not bother the other fish and is itself a powerful sport fish that is also delicious to eat.

> In nature there are neither rewards nor punishments; there are only consequences.
> —ROBERT INGERSOLL

We try to be constantly aware that when we interfere with one natural condition we risk upsetting another. Fortunately, because we are planning for the overall environment rather than for a single problem, we are able to find the lowest-risk courses of action and the ones closest to nature's methods. In all of these examples of applied systems dynamics we do not view the specific solutions as isolated events—each is part of the total system.

> And science, we should insist, better than any other discipline, can hold up to its students and followers an ideal of patient devotion to the search for objective truth, with vision unclouded by personal or political motive.
> —SIR H. H. DALT

We have been able to progress a great distance largely because, in addition to our technical knowhow, we have applied certain principles of constructive human behavior in achieving a balance between self-interest and mutual interest. It is the way we can make cool heads and warm hearts prevail in guiding our other human assets and our complex technology so that ultimately things turn out right.

> For I dipt into the future, far as human eye could see.
>
> —ALFRED, LORD TENNYSON

CHAPTER VII

Progeny

Civilization is a race between education and catastrophe.

—H. G. WELLS

THE Excelsior Log Building was only a five-block walk
down from my hotel. Fifteen years ago this beautiful mall had
been our most congested street. Central Avenue was now completely closed to street-level vehicular traffic, its people pods
moving silently overhead along the sides of the buildings.
Walking along the mall, I was aware of the existence of the
rapid transit only when passing an entrance to an underground
station.

All our knowledge has its origins in our percep-
tions.

—LEONARDO DA VINCI

For the first time since my return to the city I slowed my
pace to enjoy Excelsior Center for its own sake. I realized
that in my eagerness to gather information about specific aspects of the city my perception had narrowed so that I was not
experiencing the totality of the new environment. Now I
opened my eyes and my mind and there it was: Sol Ayre's
power, Harold Foresight's people, Marv Ellis's progress. At
this moment I realized more fully what they had been trying to

tell me—"A total system is greater than the sum of its parts"— not just a mathematical truth, but an aesthetic and emotional experience. As I looked at the attractive panorama of rooftop solar collectors, my mind's eye visualized electrical energy lighting and heating the homes of Excelsior City, powering the people-moving transit system, and freeing hydrogen to become clean-burning automobile fuel. As I turned my gaze toward the blue sky I experienced the exhilarating effect of clean, clear air, and fragrant flowers growing in the beds along the mall. As I listened to the soft sounds of a city that had become truly civilized, I appreciated the meaning of authentic human progress.

> People should think things out fresh and not just accept conventional terms and the conventional way of doing things.
> —R. BUCKMINSTER FULLER

In Excelsior City the dynamic aspects of the human personality and the physical environment had been integrated. Technology had been humanized and progress, true progress, had become a reality. I looked at the amiable faces of those around me. The people had changed the city, and the city had changed the people.

> Men come together in cities in order to live: They remain together in order to live the good life.
> —ARISTOTLE

The Excelsior Log Building was one of the Central City buildings that had been restored to its original appearance to maintain a warmth and texture in the architecture of the city. The familiar facade welcomed me as I climbed the worn marble steps to the entrance. I knew that inside I would find the polished oak banisters and paneled rooms. The *Excelsior Daily Log* was a progressive newspaper with energetic and aggressive staff members, but they voted unanimously to perpetuate the atmosphere of the original office surroundings, in which many of them had grown up. I sensed the tradition and loving care that had been lavished on the old building as I climbed the staircase to the city room on the second floor.

> To build may have to be the slow and laborious task of years. To destroy can be the thoughtless act of a single day.
> —WINSTON CHURCHILL

Recalling Eve Olve's articles about education, I began speculating about the differences between bringing up children in the Central City of today and the inner-city of 1975. Still thinking about children and the new environment of 1990, I made my way down the hall to Eve Olve's office. I looked forward to this interview with particular anticipation because Eve Olve's columns had been a powerful influence in the shaping of public opinion about, and in gaining support for, education.

> All who have meditated on the art of governing mankind have been convinced that the fate of empires depends on the education of youth.
> —ARISTOTLE

As I entered her office I was struck by its orderliness. My previous visits with journalists had led me to expect a state of organized chaos. To my delight, Eve Olve was charming and attractive and had she been a candidate for Ms. Fourth Estate of 1990, I would gladly have stuffed the ballot box in her behalf.

I told Eve that I wanted to obtain an overview of changes that had taken place in Excelsior City schools during my fifteen years' absence. She responded by relating some stories from her own school days. She considered her own experiences to be fairly typical of students who started their formal education at Excelsior Elementary School back in the mid-1950s. She felt that she had had her share of good, mediocre, and incompetent teachers. Her first-grade teacher, Adrena Lynne,

To my delight Eve Olve was charming and attractive.

was an enthusiastic teacher who made learning fun. Before long, Eve was reading and writing and regularly experiencing the joys of learning. When she reached the intermediate grades she was an avid reader and an accomplished writer, for her age. Her English teacher, Rudy Ments, helped her master the fundamentals of composition so that Eve was a proficient writer by the time she graduated from elementary school. Her secondary school English teachers, Hew Moore and Owen Mann, continued the development of her literary talents. Her music teachers were equally inspiring so that in high school she was able to qualify for membership in the top choir conducted by Bertha D. Blues.

> Education is helping the child realize his potentialities.
>
> —ERICH FROMM

Eve was not as fortunate in mathematics and science. Her

first teacher, Bea Little, sarcastically ridiculed children who made errors and her high school math teacher, Ted E. Yuss, assigned hours of repetitious homework. Her elementary science teacher, Kitty Litter, was a kindly person but was such an avid animal lover that she ignored many of the biological facts so that scientific concepts were distorted and presented irrationally.

> Those who can, do; those who can't, teach.
> —GEORGE BERNARD SHAW

Literature and writing had become such a passion with Eve that she decided to become a teacher of English. At college her study of English still delighted her, but her teacher education courses were disappointing. She endured the psychology course, consisting of theories that had little relevance to teaching; the methods courses in which she had to listen to endless tales about her instructor's experiences of thirty years ago; and practice teaching under the direction of Marge Inn, who was preoccupied with neatness, width of margins, and the evenness of the window shades in the classroom.

> There are only two places in our world where time
> takes precedence over the job to be done, school
> and prison.
> —WILLIAM GLASSER

During Eve's first year of teaching at Excelsior Central High, she discovered that very little of what she had studied at the college of education was of any practical value in the classroom. In discussions with other teachers she found that they too had to learn how to teach after graduation.

> In teaching it is the method and not the content
> that is the message . . . the drawing out, not the
> pumping in.
> —ASHLEY MONTAGU

Eve was well liked and had satisfactory relationships with

her pupils. She was successful with the students who were interested in literature, but unfortunately in this inner-city high school, with its culturally disadvantaged pupils, few were able to read, let alone appreciate the prescribed English literature.

> America is the best half-educated country in the world.
> —NICHOLAS MURRAY BUTLER

Sue Crumb, an old-time faculty member of Excelsior Central High, advised Eve not to worry about the pupils, just keep them busy and maintain order in the classroom. Jack U. Larr suggested that she entertain her pupils with jokes, field trips, and motion pictures. Eve could not accept this advice. She had not become a teacher to waste pupils' time nor to be a clown. Eve knew that the truly competent teacher, past and present, had stimulated the interest, curiosity, and affection of their pupils, but being stimulating and popular were only part of being a good teacher. She was aware of the sad fact that some of the best-liked teachers had not directed that affection to the learning of subject matter. The highly competent teacher was engaged constantly in stimulating student interest in the essential facts, concepts, insights, and attitudes required for mastery of subject matter. Eve was also aware of the fact that she had a long way to go to achieve the competencies this complex role required.

> That there should one man die ignorant who had capacity for knowledge, this I call a tragedy.
> —THOMAS CARLYLE

In spite of her earlier disappointment with teacher education courses, when a new program was offered for teachers of the culturally disadvantaged, Eve enrolled. The basic premise of the program was that teachers had middle-class values and therefore did not understand lower-class children. The content of the course consisted of sociology, cultural anthropology, ethnology, and African history. Although Eve found the course interesting, she left the program convinced that sociologists, cultural anthropologists, and African historians knew very little about how to teach an inner-city black child.

> Nothing in education is so astonishing as the amount of ignorance it accumulates in the form of inert facts.
>
> —HENRY ADAMS

Eve was a competent scholar so her professors encouraged her to continue in graduate school and obtain a doctorate. Eve was flattered but was, by now, cautious about getting involved in further courses that were irrelevant to improvement of her competencies for teaching. After looking up the doctoral dissertations of her own professors, she abandoned the idea of further graduate work in education. Dr. Dick Tater's thesis was "A Survey of Attitudes of Secondary School Principals to Questionnaires," a study in which he had sent out questionnaires to 500 principals asking them how they felt about filling out questionnaires. Dr. Fay Lure had done a study indicating that lectures were an ineffective means of educating student teachers and had since enhanced her reputation by giving lectures about her research proving the ineffectiveness of lectures.

> The average Ph.D. thesis is nothing but the transference of bones from one graveyard to another.
>
> —J. FRANK DOBIE

It was at this point that Eve started writing articles for the *Excelsior Log* about the sad state of teacher education and the irrelevance of the qualifications of those who were attempting to teach the teachers how to teach. Her first columns were eloquent pleas for equitable education for all children, improved financing of education, effective utilization of advanced technology in teaching, and early childhood education. But Eve also insisted that improved financing, better facilities, and modern technology in the hands of poorly qualified or incompetent educators could be like giving an incompetent carpenter sharper tools and more powerful equipment with which to create greater havoc.

> Emerson advised his fellow townsmen to manufacture schoolteachers and make them the best in the world.
>
> Van Wyck Brooks

Eve wrote that improvement of teacher performance through more effective teacher preparation was an essential ingredient in the solution of most educational problems and that successful teachers owed their effectiveness to their teaching experience, professional dedication, and natural gifts rather than to their professional courses. For too long teacher education had relied on the approach that says, "teachers are born, not made," or "teaching is an unspecified natural ability." Eve's articles embraced the concept that success in teaching, like success in medicine, architecture, or other professions requires certain natural aptitudes, but that success also depends on precise knowledge and skill that must be acquired.

> Not only is there an art in knowing a thing, but also a certain art in teaching it.
>
> —Cicero

Back in the early 1970s public schools were in a state of great confusion, but Eve tried to clarify the situation by describing three basic educational trends. For many years there had been two major philosophical positions in American education, although in practice most public education was a confusing mixture of both. One educational tradition was based on the idea of the importance of the three Rs and other basic content. The other tradition was called, variously, progressive, free school, child-centered, open classroom, or permissive education, and emphasized the child's subjective experience. Most teachers and educational leaders tended to fall into one or the other of these two camps.

> In all sincerity the school boards come to the conclusion that those schools will best perform their rightful task which turn out students with attitudes like their own.
>
> —H. A. OVERSTREET

Traditionalists believed that children learned responsibility by learning to conform to the teachings of the past. They talked a great deal about children learning responsibility and respect. The respect they demanded was respect for teachers and other authorities and the responsibility they expected was for the child to toe the line.

> Most subjects at universities are taught for no other purpose than they may be retaught when the students become teachers.
>
> —G. C. LICHTENBERG

The other group, progressive educators, believed in permissiveness. They thought that the educational system was somewhat irrelevant to life, so there should not be a formal educational system, as such. They encouraged the children to rap about their feelings and discuss the here-and-now, rather than making them learn about the past. One group tended to produce conformists, and the other tended to produce articulate critics and "againsters." Neither group could make education relevant enough to provide the students with the tools they needed to solve problems in the real world.

> It is neither right nor possible to think of schools and academic learning as something apart from the life of the people and of the community which the educational system is supposed to serve.
>
> —JOHN ANTHONY SCOTT

In the late 1960s, a third educational trend emerged. It started with a move toward more accountability in public education. This meant a more careful examination of the objectives of education, and descriptions of the specific competencies the students should acquire. This movement was just underway when the great environmental issues arose. The old ideas about man conquering nature, the separateness of courses of study, the survival potential of great military might, the value of competition, and the advantages of population growth had become obsolete as means of survival. Teaching for survival required acceptance of a new set of values that included man as part of nature, the interrelatedness of all knowledge, the survival potential of cooperation between individuals and nations, and the disadvantages of population growth. Education for survival should, collectively and individually, reduce selfish exploitation in favor of selfless conservation.

> Either we will eliminate pollution from our cities,
> or pollution will eliminate the cities.
> —ROBERT F. KENNEDY

Eve went on to explain the changes that took place as a result of improvement in competency-based teacher education, more accountability in public education, and the shift toward teaching for survival. Students and teachers became involved in identifying and sharing the objectives of education and in sharing much more in the evaluation process, so that students became more self-evaluative. By 1980, most students in Excelsior High School could identify a research assignment, essay, or other project and could describe the objectives for their work as well as the criteria for assessing its success. Through learning how to evaluate how well the criteria were being achieved the pupils were acquiring the essential skills of independent scholarship. In a changing world, continuous learning and independent scholarship are great assets both professionally and personally.

> In the education of children there is nothing like
> alluring the interest and affection; otherwise you
> only make so many asses laden with books.
>
> —MONTAIGNE

Another goal of competency-based teaching was to clarify the difference between basic educational objectives and individual objectives. Through involvement of teachers, parents, and educational researchers, a list of essential objectives for each course was developed. These objectives established a minimum standard that everyone in the course should meet in order to graduate. One of the benefits of defining the objectives that were essential for all children was that educators were then able to apply high-powered technology to teaching basics such as reading and writing. Audio-visual presentations, teaching machines, and individual computerized instruction provided maximum assistance for each pupil in achieving the basic educational objectives. This freed the teacher from the repetitious aspects of teaching which, in the past, had monopolized much of the teacher's time.

> The great end of education is to discipline rather
> than furnish the mind; to train it to use its own
> powers, rather than to fill it with the accumula-
> tion of others.
>
> —TYRON EDWARDS

Because children differ greatly in their interests and abilities, they were allowed to select activities of their own choice once an essential objective was achieved. This allowed each student to be as creative as he or she wished in choosing additional activities or projects. In practice this meant that as soon as a child completed an assigned task. he or she could engage in any of a wide variety of high-interest optional activities. By following the completion of an essential learning task with a satisfying activity of the child's own choosing, the essential learning was strengthened or reinforced.

> Grandma's Law: Eat your vegetables and then you can have your dessert.

This way of teaching had many desirable outcomes. Every child experienced success and satisfaction many times throughout the school day. All children mastered the fundamental learning skills—they could read and write and use these skills in independent study. Reinforcing or satisfying consequences became associated with learning so that children loved to learn. Beyond the achievement of essential skills, children learned to be creative and make their own choices.

> The supreme end of education is expert discernment in all things—the power to tell the good from the bad, the genuine from the counterfeit, and to prefer the good and genuine to the bad and the counterfeit.
>
> —SAMUEL JOHNSON

Before 1975 there had been a great deal of talk about *relevance* in education. Most of the efforts in that direction had been fragmented. Concern for human survival provided an effective incentive so that significant progress had been made in achieving educational relevance.

> The job of the teacher is to excite in the young a boundless sense of curiosity about life, so that the growing child shall come to apprehend it with an excitement tempered by awe and wonder.
>
> —JOHN GARRETT

Teachers and students developed their awareness of the environment through activities that sharpened their sensory responsiveness. For example, when literature describing environmental problems was studied, the children augmented their reading by activities that stimulated acuteness of their senses. They were encouraged to see, smell, touch, and taste the things about which they read. In this way they escaped the confines and isolation of the classroom and the symbolic or imaginary environment of textbook, motion picture, and television. By involving all of their senses, children became aware of the reality of environmental pollution and destruction as well as of the beauties of clean and natural environments.

> Our senses were made for the environment; there
> is nothing else of which they can be aware.
> —MARK TERRY

Sensitivity, awareness, and concern were only of educational value if the students could do something about what they perceived. Elevated levels of awareness motivated pupils to become involved in solving problems, but it required competence to actually be effective. Therefore pupils were encouraged to become aware of and to tackle the environmental problems right at hand in their homes, at school, and eventually in their community.

> The principal function of every artist is to make
> us see the world that was always there but which
> we were unaware of until he opened our eyes.
> —GARRETT HARDIN

An increasing variety of relevant student competencies was developed. Students brought environmental samples to science class and learned how to perform chemical and physical analysis. In this way, they learned the scientific method of problem-solving, as well as the degree of pollution in their environment. They then used their creativity and budding research skills in the search for solutions. Of course children were not encouraged to feel responsible for the destructive environmental relationship established by their elders and predecessors, nor were they expected to accept the unrealistic responsibility of stopping all pollution. But when the enthusiasm, creativity, and energy of youth were focused on a problem, solutions emerged that adults had not envisioned.

> The one-eyed mollusc on the sea bottom, feathered and luminous, is my equal in what he and I know of star clusters not yet found by the best of star gazers.
>
> —CARL SANDBURG

One way in which education fostered this new creativity was through exploring the interconnectedness of environmental conditions and the complexity of real solutions. By encouraging students to use their acquired knowledge and skills, from a number of areas of study in attacking a problem, they frequently produced unique remedies.

> It ought now be apparent that the interrelationship of our environmental problems with all other aspects of our lives is such that, if students are to understand the nature of these problems, the isolation wards which subject-area specialists have built around themselves will have to be torn down.
>
> —FORBES BOTTOMLY

Eve illustrated how students became involved in problem-solving by describing a project that included civics, psychology, and industrial arts. Excelsior City had conducted an anti-litter campaign and established a recycling center, but many adults and children still littered. A group of high school students decided to explore a practical means of getting people to put trash in the appropriate refuse containers.

The students conducted a study and came to several conclusions: (1) nonlittering was usually established during the child's formative years and was a persistent behavior pattern; (2) availability of refuse containers was a contributing factor to nonlittering, but was not the critical factor—because non-litterers would carry their refuse long distances rather than litter, while litterers would drop their trash anywhere, even a few feet from a container; (3) Excelsior Elementary School had a very effective program for training children to be litterers. As a matter of fact, at Excelsior Elementary School, a punishment for rule breakers was to have them pick up litter. By making punishment out of something that should be responsible social behavior, the school was unwittingly making it something to be avoided.

The high school students applied their knowledge of reinforcement principles by installing tape recorders in the tops of some trash containers constructed in the shape of garbage-eating critters. From the beginning, the experiment was a success. The first child who passed one of the new containers happened to be eating an apple. She paused to admire the smiling critter and fed it her apple core. This activated the tape recorder, and a pleasant, soft voice from inside the critter thanked her.

It was not long before nonlittering was established as the dominant pattern.

From the beginning the experiment was a success.

The students were so encouraged by the results of their first anti-littering experiment that they attempted a more complex project—an automated collection center for bottles, cans, and newspapers.

To work the machine all one had to do was push the start button and feed bottles, cans, and newspapers into the appropriate openings. The machine counted the bottles, sorted the aluminum and tin cans magnetically, and weighed the newspapers. It computed the total cash value and dropped the money into the cash return tray. The advantages of this collector were in its immediate cash reward and its ability to operate round-the-clock if placed in a supermarket parking lot or other easy-access location.

> Creativity is so delicate a flower that praise tends
> to make it bloom, while discouragement often nips
> it in the bud. Any of us will put out more and
> better ideas if our efforts are appreciated.
> —ALEX F. OSBORN

The machine computed the value of cans, bottles, and papers.

In concluding the interview, Eve talked about the dominant trends of fifteen years of educational progress and how these trends were interrelated. Improvements in teacher education had produced competencies for teaching that resulted in success-oriented classrooms where young people could engage in creative solving of relevant problems.

> Too often we give children answers to remember
> rather than problems to solve.
>
> —ROGER LEWIN

In 1990, the schools were still experimenting with new materials and ways to make more effective use of community resources, but the past fifteen years had been witness to substantial progress in the eradication of racism, poverty, and war —progress in which education had contributed an indispensable part.

> Public education is of key importance in educating young people to understand the realities of the world they will inherit, and to change it, not for the sake of change, but because we will not survive without change.
>
> —EVE OLVE

CHAPTER VIII

Politics

Of all sciences, there is none where first appearances are more deceitful than in politics.
— DAVID HUME

Lu CID, the famous political historian, lives in the suburbs of Excelsior City when she is not in Washington. Her country cottage is her home and office. When I visited her there, I found her to be a most energetic and delightful woman, eager to discuss her work on the President's Commission on Constitutional Reform. Her study, where we talked, was like an extension of herself. Instead of academic mustiness and gloom, the room was flooded with sunlight from the large windows that looked out onto a lovely country garden of trees and flowers.

The entire room was a pleasing disarray of books, notebooks, and papers, dominated by a large vase of freshly cut pink verbena and ferns. Next to my chair was a massive bookcase in which I noticed an interesting variety of titles—*Mountains from Molehills: Political Indiscretions and Their Consequences; Shade Ferns; Roads to Roam; Romance of the Novel; Culinary Arts á la Français; Studies in Political Congruence; Sovereignty and Common Purpose;* and *Chariot of the Frauds: Or You Can Fool All of the People.* The latter three were her own works.

The Peter Planet

I visited her in her country cottage.

> The true university of these days is a collection of
> books.
>   —THOMAS CARLYLE

We talked for a while about her books and the political strategies with which she had been associated. Political action cannot solve everything, she reminded me. For example, in the case of DDT, extravagant damage had been done before it was banned by law. DDT did kill the pests that destroyed the crops but the spray also killed the pests' natural enemies. By the time the pests had developed immunity to DDT, nature had lost its capability to control them. Then it was discovered that DDT had entered the food chain and was accumulating in the fatty tissue of fish, birds, animals, and humans.

> Recently another threat to the polar bear has been
> discovered, namely, that polar bears of the Cana-
> dian arctic carry a high concentration of DDT.
> Because they are at the end of a food chain, this

discovery is significant, showing how far the poisoning with toxic chemicals has gone. The polar bears of the arctic are, in this respect, a parallel to the DDT-contaminated penguins of the Antarctic.
—KAI CURRY-LINDAHL

The chemical companies, of course, predicted disaster for agriculture if DDT was banned. But when the farmers actually had to cope with the ban, they worked out an excellent natural solution. They returned to an old practice of timing planting and harvesting to avoid the worst periods of infestation, and the Agriculture Department introduced beneficent predators into the area. In this case, outlawing DDT did not in itself solve the problem, but it forced the farmers and agriculturists to use a less environmentally damaging means of controlling pests. The method they selected also fitted into a total systems approach, because it did not produce the disastrous side effects of DDT. The biological control of many pests has improved the yield of the crops without poisoning the environment. In the South, screwworms were a plague on livestock, but through sterilization of the male screwworms so that they engaged in a lot of nonproductive mating, the screwworm population has dropped. By coating chips of wood with a synthetic sex odor of female gypsy moths the baffled males wear themselves out having sex with the chips instead of the lady moths. The recorded love songs of female mosquitoes have been used to lure the lovesick males to their death on electric grids.

In Excelsior Forest, Clear Cut Logging had replanted the logged off area with young trees and since there were no longer any old decaying and hollow trees, nesting boxes were provided for the birds that keep under control the insect populations destructive to trees.

> Environmental concerns are no longer the private preserve of the birdwatchers: the same bell tolls for us all.
> —FRANK M. POTTER, JR.

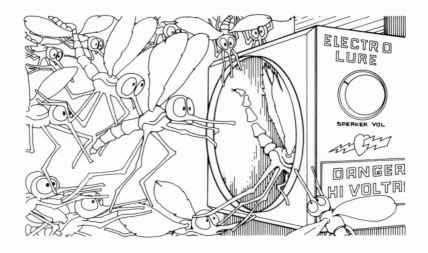

Recorded love songs lured them to their deaths.

Politicians do not have the knowledge and skills of scientists, engineers, or technicians. Sometimes, however, by simply outlawing a harmful substance the lawmakers can set a creative process in motion that leads to a better solution.

> The universe is full of magical things patiently
> waiting for our wits to grow sharper.
> —EDEN PHILLPOTTS

Another way in which legislators can stimulate the creation of solutions is through the imposition of penalties. For example, they can force polluters to be financially responsible for damage to the environment. Whatever they mess up, they pay to clean up. Restrictive and punitive methods can be effective as long as there is a constructive way out of the problem. If a person or a company has to pay the full social and economic cost of pollution, they often find a way to stop it. Until a non-polluting system is operating, a pollution tax based on the pay-as-you-pollute principle can be used to help clean up the environment. The pay-as-you-pollute principle will work only where it creates a situation that causes the pollutor, in his best self-interest, to change his ways.

> Nothing astonishes men so much as common sense and plain dealing.
>
> —R. W. EMERSON

The pollution of Excelsior Lake from Polyglot Chemicals' waste products dumped into the water turned a once-beautiful lake into an ecological tragedy. The oxygen content was depleted, aquatic vegetation died, algae multiplied, the water turned to muck, and the fish succumbed. It was not easy to assess the value of the loss to society caused by this kind of pollution. The council imposed a tax that was a compromise between the cost of rehabilitating the lake, the estimated value to society of the source of pure water, recreation that was lost as a result of the damage to the lake, and the amount that would make it financially feasible for Polyglot to unfoul its nest. Polyglot was presented with a tax bill per unit of solid, liquid, or heat pollution. Apparently the penalty was stiff enough that Polyglot became ecology-minded. Now, rather than letting heated water flow directly into the lake, it is delivered to cooling ponds. Catfish, an excellent source of high-quality protein, grow exceptionally well in warm water. Sale of the catfish raised in the cooling ponds helped pay off the cost of reducing heat pollution of the lake. Hot discharge water for warmer fish-farming ponds and bigger fish have become a standard practice in many areas of the country. Also recently, warm water irrigation has been used to make vegetation germinate and grow more rapidly in Excelsior Valley and elsewhere.

> It is not from the benevolence of butcher, the brewer, or the baker that we expect our dinner, but from their regard to their own interest.
>
> —ADAM SMITH

In time, the other waste products that had been dumped into Excelsior Lake were removed through filtration, sedimentation, and biochemical means, and Polyglot no longer must pay a lake pollution tax. This illustrates how the pay-as-you-pollute tax works without forcing the government to impose a bureaucratic solution on the offending polluter. This also illustrates how technology, used improperly, can get us into trouble and how technology, used properly, can get us out of trouble.

> The translation of values into public policy is what
> politics is about.
>
> —WILLARD GAYLIN

The objection to governmentally imposed restrictions or punishments is that they sometimes result in avoidance behavior. Polyglot Chemicals could have tried to avoid the pollution tax by threatening to go out of business, thus creating an unemployment problem. It could have tried to use lobbyists and contributions to buy political influence to delay enforcement of the pay-as-you-pollute tax. It could have tried any number of ways to avoid the penalty, other than the constructive one it chose.

> Government is necessary, not because man is natu-
> rally bad, but because man is by nature more in-
> dividualistic than social.
>
> —THOMAS HOBBES

There are situations in which the government should establish objectives and reward individuals or companies that achieve the objectives. This positive reinforcement approach does not produce any of the avoidance of restrictive and punitive methods. For example, in the late 1960s, the government established emission control standards for the automobile industry. The industry claimed the standards were too high and engaged in delaying maneuvers. They obtained a series of postponements so that enforcement of the emission standards was delayed for several years. Eventually, the government offered an attractive financial reward in the form of tax incentives to the purchasers of low-polluting or nonpolluting automobiles. There was no avoidance response to the combination of rewards for nonpolluting stock model cars (including the special purchase tax on every polluting car sold) along with the reduced license fees for owners of nonpolluting vehicles.

> Strong reasons make strong actions.
> —W. SHAKESPEARE

When politicians know what is needed, they should enact legislation that clearly states the objective and the rewards available. The effectiveness of this positive approach has been proven time and again. The old approach—restrictions, fines, imprisonment—is still necessary to discourage socially dangerous behavior. These restrictive laws help to keep some undesirable behavior under control, but they do little to encourage desirable behavior.

> In the search for ways to maintain our values
> and pursue them in an orderly way, we must
> look beyond the resources of law.
> —DEAN ACHESON

Our political system was originally developed to protect individual rights and state rights. The Constitution was not conceived with foreknowledge of the fearful threat technology would become in 200 years. It gave our traditional institutions of government no means of controlling a runaway technology that would eventually threaten our very existence.

> We have broken out of the circle of life, converting
> its endless cycles into man-made linear events.
> —BARRY COMMONER

The ultimate effect of a political decision is not usually

The Peter Planet

obvious at the time it is made. In some cases it may be twenty
years or more before its full effect can be weighed. In terms of
long-range human survival, our elected officials have very
limited knowledge of ecosystems and the complex consequences of the changes we impose on the environment.

Back in the early 1970s, pollsters took the pulse of the public every week to see how the President and the government
were doing. If the President's popularity was up three points
the news media proclaimed that confidence in the executive
branch had been restored, and when it dropped two points,
that public trust was being eroded. This kind of short-term
popularity contest supported the political opportunist who best
reflected the public whim of the moment. Stopgap measures to
curb inflation, provide more fuel, or settle a dispute can actually result in compounding problems for the future.

> *Americanism* is a damn good word with which
> to carry an election.
> —WARREN HARDING

A leader has more opportunities to see further down the
road than the rest of us. The competent leader must have long-
range vision, and be able to see not only through his own eyes
but through the eyes of others. This is particularly important
in an age when many political decisions should be based on
information from a variety of specialists.

> Everybody is ignorant, only on different subjects.
> —WILL ROGERS

Back in 1975, there was a lot of confusion between being
"in charge" and being "a leader." One can be in charge as long
as one holds office, but being a competent leader requires
more. The higher the office, the further one should see.

> Leaders are the custodians of a nation's ideals,
> of the beliefs it cherishes, of its permanent hopes,

of the faith which makes a nation out of an aggre-
gation of individuals.

—WALTER LIPPMANN

Political debate, bureaucratic red tape, commissions, grants-in-aid to special interest groups—no matter how well intentioned—were actually the fragmentation of solutions rather than whole solutions. Only the futurists, using sophisticated technology, were able to accumulate all the known factors about the earth's resources, population, and pollution, and by using computers, to make the millions of continuous calculations necessary to understand the total problem. The futurists of 1975 could see a series of computer graphs all presenting a mathematical picture of impending disaster. The competent futurists, scientists, systems analysts, social engineers, and ecologists understood the interrelatedness of the components of our dilemma. Application of systems dynamics offered the

The higher the office, the further one should see.

only overall, rational way to find lasting solutions based on enormous quantities of incredibly complex and continuously changing information. Through the application of systems dynamics and computer simulation we could predict results at the time political decisions were being made.

> If we are to be effective, we are going to have to think in both the biggest and most minutely incisive ways permitted by intellect and by the information thus far won through experience.
> —R. BUCKMINSTER FULLER

In 1975 the most difficult political change we had to make was a fundamental change in the attitudes of Americans toward the problems that faced their nation. Although the future looked bleak in 1975, it was essential that the pessimistic view not be allowed to prevail. Intelligent steps had to be taken to gain control over runaway destructive forces. This required a genuine belief that the emerging crises in the economy, environment, population, and international relations were not predestined.

> It is certainly wrong to despair; and if despair is wrong hope is right.
> —JOHN LUBBOCK

The pessimism of the early 1970s was a product of the failure of the short-term crisis management policies of our government. As long as resources appeared plentiful America did not have to face up to the destructive consequences of its actions. We were not compelled to consider the cost, in terms of the depletion of our own resources, of our military actions abroad. Until the energy squeeze, we were unwilling to examine the impact of our technology on our environment, and it took serious deterioration of our cities to awaken us to the undermining of family life and community organization by "welfare economics."

When you begin with much pomp and show,
Why is the end so little and so low?
—WENTWORTH D. ROSCOMMON

Lu Cid pointed out that in the early 1970s we had the necessary information and the ability to foresee these consequences, but we not only refused to do so, we rejected the advice of futurists, ecologists, and others who could have helped. By 1975 Americans were following three major social trends and each of these was reflected in the political policies of the country. The predominant mode was reflected in a hedonistic life-style and faith that stopgap measures would muddle us through our troubles and things would soon get back to normal. Although reckless crash programs to patch up the economy or overcome shortages had little prospect of reinstating the old industrial order, this group continued to try to recapture the past.

> Gerald Ford was elected by only one vote and
> nobody demanded a recount.
>
> —LU CID

A substantial number of Americans turned to mysticism. They abandoned attempts at rational thought and embraced quasi-religions, such as the Jesus Freaks or the exotic Eastern cults whose gurus professed magical insights and powers. They worshipped at the feet of pseudo-scientists who promised health and beauty through fad diets or quack treatments. They became the patients and followers of quasi-therapists who promised them relief from the human condition through encounter groups, sensitivity training, extrasensory perception, primitive screaming, exorcism, and occultism. These mystical solutions promised instant results and did not require the long, hard struggle of thinking, studying, and reasoning. All of these fads diverted attention from reality.

> The Constitution gives every American the in-
> alienable right to make a damn fool of himself.
>
> —JOHN CIARDI

A third group realized the futility of both the "business as usual" and the "faith healing" approach. This group did not believe that there was an easy way out of our troubles but they believed there was a way out. They worked on conversion strategies that would eventually produce a society of compatible elements for survival of human civilization. These conversion strategies included development of nonpolluting energy sources. The Sol Ayre Solar Farm was not the be-all and end-all of energy development, but it was an essential step in the shift from reliance on oil imports, high-sulphur coal, and the race to exploit offshore reserves. Harold Foresight's concept of civilian service for Excelsior City led to establishment of a network of Centers for Civilian Service. These centers studied community needs and the unemployed themselves were involved in deciding how their energies and abilities could best be put to work in fulfilling these needs. Unemployed scientists, engineers, and technicians created programs for building, renovation, and so forth. The Centers for Civilian Service elicited enormous amounts of human creativity, provided jobs, and deployed human energy to critical problem areas without establishing huge, stultifying bureaucracies.

> More with less.
> —R. Buckminster Fuller

Although those who tried to return to the old economics and those who sought instant solutions still persisted, the numbers of those who worked for rational humanistic alternatives increased. Lu Cid believed that if they had not, the pessimists' predictions would have been fulfilled.

By the time my interview with Lu Cid was over it was late afternoon. As I made my departure she accompanied me through her garden, picking some flowers for me to take to my hotel room.

> The longer I live the more beautiful life becomes.
> The earth's beauty grows on men. If you foolishly

Lu Cid exemplified beauty in thought and deed.

ignore beauty, you'll soon find yourself without it.
Your life will be impoverished, But if you wisely
invest in beauty, it will remain with you all the
days of your life.

—FRANK LLOYD WRIGHT

CHAPTER IX

Peace

> If an international controversy leads to armed con-
> flict, everyone loses; if armed conflict is avoided,
> everyone wins. It is better to lose a point now and
> then in an international tribunal and gain a world
> in which everyone lives at peace under the rule of
> law.
>
> —DWIGHT D. EISENHOWER

FOR this final interivew, I was back on the campus of Excelsior College, visiting the director of the Peace Research
Center. A large painting of the Dove of Peace dominated the
office of Frank A. Praisal. His gentle manner and soft voice
belied the fact that he was an ardent crusader. When I asked
him for his appraisal of the progress that had been made toward world peace, he gave me his version of history.

> We are all citizens of history.
> —CLIFTON FADIMAN

He began by stating that in all of recorded history, there
have been only about 200 years when the world was free from
war. The earliest known picture of man was recently discovered scratched on the wall of an ancient cave and it was a
picture of men clubbing each other to death.

He always had a chip on his shoulder that he was
ready to use to kindle an argument.
                                    —FRED ALLEN

Sometime early in our development, man began the noble
experiment of becoming civilized. He started with the making
of tools, which led to specialization and the restructuring of
tribal life. Some members of the tribe became the hunters, while
others were more suited to being food gatherers, herdsmen, and
toolmakers. Specialization required that rules be established
for the sharing of food, shelter, and tribal wealth. Usually a
dominant male took over the position of chief and along with
the elders of the tribe made and enforced the rules. The central responsibility of the chief and the elders was the preservation of tribal structure and order. Offenders against the rules
were brought before the chief and elders. After a hearing they
handed down a judgment, and the offender was punished,

A large painting of the Dove of Peace dominated the office.

Early man.

executed, expelled from the tribe, or placed under a spell or curse. From our modern legal point of view, we might disagree with the justice of the decisions and the punishments, but it was a system of law, and it worked pretty well.

> As to capital punishment: If it was good enough
> for my father, it's good enough for me.
> —VICTOR MOORE

Tribes originally occupied relatively isolated locations where life support was plentiful. As time passed groups of tribal members became separated and learned to exist in harsh environments where life support was minimal. Some tribes split up because they populated beyond the local capacity of their environment. They depleted the game and destroyed the vegetation. Others left because of changes of climate, new insects, diseases and other natural foes, or because of invasions by enemy tribes. Tribes that stayed in one area as long as they could often had to adapt to a deteriorating environment and those that left frequently found themselves, eventually, in similar circumstances.

> The fouling of the nest, which has been typical of man's activity in the past on a local scale, now seems to be extending to the whole system.
> —KENNETH BOUDLING

As tribes adapted to their territories, some hunted, some fished, some gathered food from the plants and trees, and some grew their own crops and domesticated the animals from the wilds. Although a tribe might be aware of a neighboring tribe's existence, prehistoric man was ignorant of the vast variety of the earth's resources.

> To be ignorant of one's ignorance is the malady of the ignorant.
> —BRONSON ALCOTT

When hunters from one tribe happened upon a neighboring tribe's store of food, they took it. If they met with resistance, they used their hunting clubs and spears as weapons. To the victor went the spoils of battle. Might *was* right. Eventually a new specialization was born—that of soldier. With military might, tribes weren't limited to just stealing their neighbor's food, they could also acquire desirable territories by capturing or killing their neighbors. This worked pretty well for the winners.

> Nothing should be left to an invaded people except their eyes for weeping.
> —BISMARCK

Some of the more inventive and adventurous built rafts for exploration and fishing in local rivers and bays. As they built bigger rafts, dugouts, and boats they ventured out to sea. It was only a matter of time before they had ships carrying sea-men-warriors who robbed, conquered, and raped the peoples of distant lands. This, too, worked pretty well and the seamen-warriors, along with the kings who commissioned their adventures, prospered.

> The proof that man is the noblest of all creatures
> is that no other creature has ever denied it.
> —G. C. LICHTENBERG

In time some tribes banded together in support of great shipbuilding and military enterprises. The more cunning sea-venturing warriors figured out a shortcut to fortune by plundering the plunderers—intercepting and capturing ships returning with their loot from distant lands. This also worked pretty well for the successful sea pirates.

> A little thieving is a dangerous art,
> But thieving largely is a noble part;
> 'Tis vile to rob a henroost of a hen,
> But stealing largely makes us gentlemen.
> —SAMUEL S. MARSHALL

The countries with the best warriors and sea pirates were invincible. They captured great quantities of valuables, territory, and slaves. The slaves were put to work growing and harvesting crops to increase the wealth of the slave owners. This worked pretty well for the slave owners.

> The most successful slave trader operating out of
> Liverpool was Sir John Hawkins. He kidnapped
> some 75,000 natives from their homes in West
> Africa. The name of his slave ship was *The Jesus*.
> —MCNEIL DIXON

Ordinary citizens never asked their leaders to send them to war. The leaders, along with their sea pirates and slave owners, were now called businessmen and industrialists and they knew that the valuable resources of the planet occurred only here and there and usually remote from each other. They convinced the citizens that the people occupying the valuable territories ought to be conquered. Ordinary citizens were trained as soldiers and sailors and went forth in their warships to kill the foreign people and capture the resources of their lands. This worked pretty well for the businessmen and industrialists and it enhanced the power of the leaders.

> War, like any other racket, pays high dividends to the very few. The cost of operations is always transferred to the people who do not profit.
> —SMEDLEY BUTLER

Modern man.

Within the national boundaries of an organized, modern territory there were laws that were usually effective. Occasionally there was a revolution or a civil war, but these were temporary internal upsets. In each country, the law was effective only up to its national borders. On the American frontier, lawlessness and gun toting flourished until law became effective. The basis of effective law was arbitration. If a frontiersman offended the law, or if two ranchers were involved in a dispute, they appeared before a judge who had authority to arbitrate the case. He would pass sentence on the offender, or hand down a binding decision to the feuding ranchers. This system of peace worked pretty well within the national boundaries of the United States.

> Where laws ends, tyranny begins.
> —WILLIAM PITT, JR.

Most of the nations of the world practiced law at home to preserve domestic peace, but still went to war abroad. Even the most culturally advanced of the great powers launched military attacks on other countries. Although the citizens of these modern countries never asked their leaders to get them involved in wars, they gave up their lives patriotically to the cause. This, too, worked pretty well for the leader, the businessmen, and the industrialists, who were now called the President and the military-industrial complex.

> The armed forces of one's own nation exist—so each nation asserts—to *prevent* aggression by other nations. But the armed forces of other nations exist—or so many people believe—to *promote* aggression.
> —BERTRAND RUSSELL

The escalation of military power to where it could overkill the population of the planet appears to be irrational, but from a psychological point of view, however, it makes apparent sense. The early tribal leaders found that by organizing their members for defense and providing them with bigger clubs or longer spears they could increase the tribe's security. The leaders, therefore, continued to escalate the size of their military establishment and the kill-power of their weapons. By the time that the military takeover of territory and the capturing of slaves no longer seemed profitable, the cost of sophisticated weapons had risen to the point where the preparation for war and the making of war were financially profitable in their own right. The fortunes of war go to the munitions manufacturers and the industrialists in support industries—on both sides. After the smoke and dust of the war has cleared away, the so-called losers may be better off economically and materially than the so-called winners, as in the case of Germany and Japan.

> Everyone knows by now that atoms that are friendly when far enough apart become fearsomely explosive when enough of them are so compressed and arranged that a stray cat called a neutron can start a chain reaction.
> —ROBERT C. WOOD

In looking back, Frank A. Praisal saw the mid-1970s as the most critical period in the history of civilization. If we had continued militarization of the world through power politics, military alliances, and mutual aid pacts, the world would still be divided into competing armed camps. If we had continued experimentation with nuclear weapons even without actually using them in combat, we would have destroyed the ozone layer and exposed all mankind to lethal levels of ultraviolet rays from the sun. By now this would have wiped us out, even if radioactive fallout had not.

> Gone are those pleasant nineteenth-century days when a country could remain neutral and at peace just by saying it wanted to.
> —WILLIAM L. SHIRER

The time had come when world peace through world law was imperative. Advancing technology had created problems for which we had no effective system of law. For example, the use of radar and other electronic devices had made it possible for a fishing fleet to locate and catch enormous quantities of fish. There was no law to stop one country from eliminating the traditional food supply of another and there was no effective protection of fish breeding areas. This technology was so efficient that baby herring—we buy them as canned sardines—were caught in such abundance that hardly any escaped to become adult breeding stock. The very existence of this traditional and valuable source of food was threatened.

Overharvesting of fish, extermination of whales, pollution, and destruction of the seabed through new methods of mining forced us to confront the issue of who owns the oceans and who should protect them.

> It's co-existence
> Or no existence.
> —BERTRAND RUSSELL

The emergence of multinational corporations presented another problem that transcended national boundaries. Without effective international law the transnationals could operate outside of the law. Globe-straddling corporations were more powerful than the governments of many nations. (For example, multinationals financed the overthrow of the government of Chile.) Not only could the multinational corporations start revolutions and wars, there were no transnational regulations to stop them from selling munitions to both sides, which they did.

> Corporations have at different times been so far unable to distinguish freedom of speech from freedom of lying that their freedom had to be curbed.
> —CARL BECKER

Frank A. Praisal was quick to point out that bigness was not necessarily badness, and that multinational corporations were neither worse nor better than national corporations. His point was that because we had not made law effective beyond national borders, transnational and globe-straddling banks and corporations were able to impose their own totalitarian regime on the world. On the other hand, if these same multi-nationals were working within a framework of international law for world peace they could be the means of solving world-wide problems and stabilizing the global economy. So long as this is a world of imperfect human beings we can't depend on the voluntary measures of self-regulation to solve our international conflicts, any more than we can expect all offenders in civil cases to volunteer to appear in court and then to abide by the decision.

> If men were angels, no government would be necessary.
> —JAMES MADISON

Frank A. Praisal then described the purpose of peace research as essentially the same as those of national defense. Military might is no longer viable national defense. Only *enforceable* law to guarantee peace offers effective national defense. The efforts of the Peace Research Center had been devoted to defining peace and developing conversion strategies for the transition from reliance on military might to reliance on enforceable law.

> Liberty! Liberty! In all things let us have justice, and then we shall have enough liberty.
> —JOSEPH JOUBERT

The Peace Research Center's six definitions of peace started with the minimum condition and progressed to the essentials for world peace.

1. Cease-fire in place.
2. Cease-fire with both sides withdrawing to lines established through arbitration.
3. Sequential world-wide arms reduction.
4. Mediation of disputes.

5. Acceptance of international law and of the World Court as the arbitrator in cases of conflict in which mediation fails to provide an acceptable resolution.

6. Acceptance of the International Peace Force as the official agency of world law enforcement.

> The most tragic paradox of our time is to be found in the failure of nation states to recognize the imperatives of internationalism.
> —EARL WARREN

The conversion strategies were developed by methods used by the military. Generals had played war games for hundreds of years and in modern times computers were used in playing simulation games. By playing peace games and using computer simulation, the problems of peace were explored realistically. The economy was so involved in the maintenance of the military that disarmament would have caused a serious economic disruption with widespread unemployment. On the other hand, the country and the world needed well-organized systematic solutions for energy, pollution, population, food, and transportation. The peace games explored what would happen when military capabilities and facilities were applied to our peaceful survival needs. Other simulations explored the emotional aspects included in the love of war and military power.

> I do like to see the arms and legs fly.
> —COLONEL GEORGE S. PATTON, III

Frank A. Praisal had been guided throughout his career by the prophecy from the book of Isaiah 2:4:

> . . . they shall beat their swords into plowshares, and their spears into pruninghooks; nation shall not lift up sword against nation, neither shall they learn war any more.

His faith in the prophecy had not deflected his efforts from the practical problems that had to be overcome in achieving a world free from war and the threat of war.

> Peace is more difficult than war. It takes two to make a peace and only one to make a war.
>   —FRANK A. PRAISAL

PART THREE

The Peter Program

However brilliant an action it should not be
esteemed great unless the result of a great motive.
—FRANÇOIS DE LA ROCHEFOUCAULD

CHAPTER X

Participation

You go on the tennis court to play tennis, not to
see if the lines are straight.
—ROBERT FROST

W HEN one reaches the edge of an abyss, the only truly
progressive move is first to step backward—and then change
course. We have explored our present dilemma and visualized
the good and sensible world we can achieve. We should now
consider the *conversion strategies* that could enable us to make
the transition from an obsolete system to a new civilization.

Acting without thinking is like shooting without
aiming.
—B. C. FORBES

Life-styles can be important in the transition from a re-
source-depletion economy to a survival economy, and es-
pecially if you are willing to adapt some of your behavior in
order to be less a part of the environmental deterioration
problem and more a part of the solution. Your personal conversion strategies may involve many aspects of your life. Take
aluminum and tin cans, newspapers, magazines, and bottles
to a recycling center and donate used clothing and household
items to a salvage organization. Give up smoking and thereby
stop polluting your air intake and that of others. Compost

garden waste and reestablish one of nature's cycles right in your own yard. Recycle an old building by repairing or remodeling it to save material and conserve the energy that would be required to manufacture new materials. Insulate your house to keep the heat in and the cold out. At your place of business, church, or social organization, provide reusable china coffee mugs rather than disposal plastic or paper cups. Plant trees that contribute to an improved environment by absorbing carbon dioxide and releasing oxygen. A tree can protect your house from excessive heat in summer and reduce your heating bill in winter while creating a quieter atmosphere for you to live in. If you buy a living Christmas tree, you can plant it in your yard or donate it to a park after the festive season is over.

Well, it looks like another Merry Christmas.

Possible personal conversion strategies cover an infinite range of human behavior, but the general principles behind these strategies are not difficult to understand. Everything we

obtain, use, and dispose of has an environmental effect somewhere so we should be aware of where things come from as
well as their ultimate fate after we have used them. Eliminate
needless consumption by avoiding throwaway products and
those designed for obsolescence.

> A principle is never useful or living or vital until
> it is embodied in an action.
>
> —MANLY HALL

One individuals' life-style based on these principles of personal responsibility will not solve the global problem of a deteriorating environment, but you can set an example that will
influence others. Millions of people not living by these principles have caused the problems and millions applying these
principles can bring about the necessary changes.

> The people, though we think of a great entity when
> we use the word, means nothing more than so
> many millions of individual men.
>
> —LORD BRYCE

There are many people and organizations that are engaged
in activities contributing to the transition of our destructive
society to a conserving civilization. Through your member-
ships, participation in, and financial support of organizations
devoted to alleviation of the problems facing our planet, you
will strengthen their influence. Your support strategies may
also include voting for individuals or political actions, writing
letters, petitioning for change, boycotting certain products and
companies, or testifying against polluters and fraudulent enterprises.

> Every man is worth just as much as the things
> are worth about which he busies himself.
>
> —MARCUS AURELIUS

Many problems can only be resolved through a total systems
approach. The present transportation problems of poor service,

fuel shortages, and pollution, cannot be dealt with effectively by treating trains, planes, ships, buses, trucks, and automobiles as competitive components. Only through developing cooperatively interacting transportation components can we achieve an efficient system. Civilization can progress beyond its present primitive disregard for waste and destruction to a more comprehensive accommodation of all of the relevant environmental components. The total systems approach is more productive, practical, and certainly less wasteful than our fragmented technology of today.

> We can be the creative architects of ecosystems
> that will serve mankind, and protect the flora and
> fauna that we want to protect, and that surely will
> be almost all of them.
>
> —SHEPHERD MEAD

Some early applications of limited ecological systems have been eminently successful. Fish hatcheries have stocked lakes and rivers and reestablished fish populations in depleted areas. Around the turn of the century, the river Thames was an open sewer. As a result of stricter controls of effluents discharged into the river, the Thames is recovering and the fish are returning. It has become standard practice in England to remove organic matter from sewage and discharge the cleaned-up water to the rivers. The treated organic material is used as fertilizer. With the expansion of this kind of system we could have pipelines from our cities that would deliver treated sewage to agricultural areas to fertilize the land, or it could be used to turn deserts into productive farmland. Future generations will look back on our sewage disposal practices much as we look back on the medieval custom of throwing excrement out the windows into the streets.

> Man shapes himself through decisions that shape
> his environment.
>
> —RENE DUBOS

By creating systems that are complete and compatible with natural ecological cycles we can improve our planet and convert it into a pleasant, permanent, and really superb place to live.

> Many of the problems the world faces today are the eventual result of short-term measures taken last century.
>
> —JAY FORRESTER

The Peter Program presents a sampling of conversion strategies that can start the system moving in a positive direction.

> The system is still us.
> —ART SEIDENBAUM

THE PETER PERSON

If we busy ourselves with the details of our own personal lives and stay in our own backyards, the immediate universe may seem fine for the moment. If we wait for someone to lead us out of the darkness into the light of a new and better day, we may find ourselves waiting forever or following self-proclaimed and unprincipled manufacturers of miracles. If we decide to wait for the government to make the first move, it may be as fruitless and disillusioning as *Waiting for Godot*.

Traditionally, we have tried to improve our lot by seeking out and blaming the evildoer. Although there is no shortage of deserving scapegoats, we must remember that the line dividing good and evil passes through the heart of every human being. The future lies in our awareness of the consequences of our deeds and our concern for our own behavior.

> There is no difference between time and any of the three dimensions of space except that our consciousness moves along it.
>
> —H. G. WELLS

The individual who commits violence in the name of Peace is already on the road to becoming that which he hates. The celebrant of Earth Day who leaves his beer cans in the grass pollutes in the name of Environment. Our ratio of emotionalism to careful analysis is perilously high. Emotion is the necessary motivating force in getting things started. Sometimes that emotion is anger, but hatred toward others becomes self-destructive and frequently counterproductive. It is natural to detest the behavior of those who are destroying our planet, but anger must be channeled constructively. We need individuals who are well-informed, disciplined, and persistently determined.

> Every man without passions has within him no
> principle of action, nor motive to act.
> —CLAUDE ANDRIEN HELVETIUS

If you will start with some of the easier problems, you will build your self-confidence and prepare yourself for tackling larger issues. It is not martyrdom, but competence and success that strengthen the will.

> Martyrs set bad examples.
> —DAVID RUSSELL

You must be willing to question the beliefs by which you were brought up, and become more fully aware that in what you do lies the future of humanity. Ultimate success will depend on your commitment to honesty, peace, and love for your planet-home.

> I know of no safe depository of the ultimate pow-
> ers of the society but the people themselves.
> —THOMAS JEFFERSON

THE PETER PURCHASER

When you visit a supermarket, an automobile agency, or an investment counselor, the choices you make will have an effect

—for better or worse—on the air you breathe, the water you drink, and on the future of us all. Your purchase shapes the future in two important ways. First, the product you buy has a direct environmental impact. It may cause environmental pollution or its manufacture may destroy irreplaceable resources. Second, when you purchase a product or service you influence the behavior of the producer of that product or service. Every time you are manipulated or flimflammed by an advertiser into buying a product, the advertiser is encouraged to continue his razzle-dazzle strategies.

> Advertising is the art of making whole lies out of
> half-truths.
> —EDGAR A. SHOAFF

We have been manipulated and hoodwinked into buying more and more goods, in a never-ending quest for the good life until we overconsume and discard to the point of destroying the source of our affluence. Through the purchase of high-quality, long-lasting products and the refusal to buy overpackaged, throwaway, or polluting products, you will persuade manufacturers to stop producing these harmful materials and to join you in partnership for survival.

> The aim is not more goods for people to buy, but
> more opportunities for them to live.
> —LEWIS MUMFORD

Fortunately, you can take positive steps to regain your self-respect as a purchaser. Demand that you be treated rationally and protest when you are not, so that you can recapture some of the old-fashioned pride of the prudent shopper.

> The race advances only by the extra achievements
> of the individual. You are the individual.
> —CHARLES TOWNE

With expanding public awareness of environmental issues, it should be easy for the purchaser to avoid products that increase pollution. Unfortunately, this is not so. Industry is quick to see the profit potential in your concerns. For example, household trash must be separated so that the materials may be recycled. This is the only rational solution to the problem. Did industry come up with a trash separator? No, it came up with a trash compactor to smash it all together in plastic-bagged blocks. Promotion of the compactor is based on the concept that the less space your trash requires, the less there is. What is to be done with the deodorized, compacted block is unclear. Locking up potentially valuable materials in compressed blocks is certainly a step in the wrong direction, although the ads say, "Fight pollution with a trash compactor—take out a week's garbage in one trip."

> Our major obligation is not to mistake slogans for solutions.
> —EDWARD R. MURROW

If you already own one of the machines, however, you can outwit "them" by deciding to compact only one kind of trash at a time. For instance, if you throw only aluminum cans into the compactor, the end product will be a marketable, recyclable aluminum block.

> There is nobody so irritating as somebody with less intelligence and more sense than we have.
> —DON HEROLD

Originally detergents were advertised as the way to make things cleaner. They cleaned our clothes and dishes but, unfortunately, dirtied our environment. They were not biodegradable. Manufacturers responded by producing "New Improved Formulas" containing additional enzymes with escalated levels of phosphates and so a new pollution problem was created.

> We live in a war of two antagonistic ethical phi-

losophies, the ethical policy taught in the books
and schools, and the success policy.
—WILLIAM GRAHAM SUMNER

As purchasers we cannot rely on advertising as a source of
dependable information. We have to make commonsense decisions based on knowledge of the products and their ingredients. Fortunately consumer reports and labels that list the
ingredients have simplified the problem of choosing nonpolluting products. The pollution solution, like charity, begins at
home.

I was confused by an ad that read: *Why go else-*
where to be cheated! You can trust us to do the job.
—STEVE STROSSER

PACKAGING Americans buy about 70 million tons of packaging materials each year, an average of about 660 pounds
of paper, plastics, glass, metal, and other packaging materials
per person. Ninety percent of it is discarded.

Willful waste brings woeful want.
—THOMAS FULLER

Without lowering the standard of living, the Peter Purchaser
can make an ecologically positive contribution through simply
reducing throwaway packaging. Paper bags are an obvious
waste of natural resources. Buy or make your own reusable
shopping bag. The stretchable net type used by European
shoppers is lightweight, strong, and durable.

Boycott no-deposit, no-return bottles. If you wish to take
further action, contact local conservation groups and write to
your legislator urging support of programs to ban disposable
bottles. Oregon, Vermont, Finland, and British Columbia, to
name a few, have all passed effective legislation to outlaw
throwaway bottles.

Paper bags are an obvious waste of natural resources.

> I can attack my government, try to organize to change it. That's more than I can do in Moscow, Peking, or Havana.
> —SAUL ALINSKY

As soon as there is a substantial trend back to returnable bottles, it would be feasible to legislate the standardization of the shape and size so that reusable bottles would not have to be sorted for brand name and a sensible, efficient shape of bottle would become universal.

> There is one thing stronger than all the armies in the world: and that is an idea whose time has come.
> —VICTOR HUGO

Manufacturers have used overpackaging as an effective psychological attack on the purchaser. By enclosing a bottle in a wrapper inside a box, which in turn is wrapped in an elegantly expensive outer wrapper, the illusion is created that the contents are of great value. Common sense tells us that no amount of outer adornment can improve the real value of the contents. Learn to counter the psychological effect of the packager's motto, "When it's tied up in tinsel it's hard to resist," by using logic and boycotting overpackaged products. If you do purchase or receive them, express your disapproval to the manufacturer. To make your point clear you might return the unnecessary packaging.

> To do something is in every man's power.
> —SAMUEL JOHNSON

POLLUTION   A great deal of unnecessary poison is released into the environment by pesticides, leaded gasoline, cleansers, and industrial wastes. If you use insecticides, make sure they are botanicals. These are short-lived plant extracts that break down into harmless compounds. Some well-known botanicals to ask for are nicotine, pyrethrum, and rotenone.

> A weed is a plant whose virtues have not yet been discovered.
> —RALPH WALDO EMERSON

The main source of lead contamination is tetraethyl lead used in gasoline. Reduce the amount of this pollutant by driving less, pooling transportation, using low-lead or no-lead gasoline, and supporting legislation to "Get The Lead Out."

> A nation without the means of reform is without means of survival.
> —EDMUND BURKE

When phosphates in detergents enter our lakes, streams, rivers, and oceans, they stimulate the growth of algae which robs the water of its oxygen and produces a poisonous gas killing fish and other aquatic life.

Select detergents with low levels of phosphate or none at all. Stop using enzyme presoaks, because they are generally

Phosphates in detergents kill fish and other aquatic life.

two-thirds phosphate. Try going back to using laundry soap instead of detergent. If your area has hard water add washing soda or borax. Clothing washed in this manner is less irritating to the skin and no fabric softener will be required.

PERMANENCE   Whenever you select a throwaway product over a reusable item you encourage the manufacturer to make more throwaways and the environment carries the burden. The average American discards 540 pounds of paper each year as our forests disappear. Use cloth napkins and towels, which can be added to other washing with negligible additional use of water and cleaner. During your lifetime you will save many trees. When you buy durable items manufacturers are encouraged to improve the quality of their products. Buy clothes and other products with an eye to long-time usefulness and suitability to you rather than those that are just a fad soon to disappear.

It is quality rather than quantity that matters.

—SENECA

PROFIT   In the field of money management, a good investment needed only to turn a profit according to tradition. If an investor balked at turning a profit by financing the military-industrial complex, pollution violators, or racist hiring organizations, he was confronted with the problem of seeking out "clean" stocks on his own. Recently, however, there has emerged a new type of mutual fund for the customer with a social conscience. For example, the Pax World Fund avoids investing in any company on the Pentagon's list of the 100 largest U.S. defense contractors, while the Dreyfus Third Century Fund ranks the firms in which it invests according to the concern they show for consumers, environment, safety, and equal opportunity, as well as observing the normal investment standards.

> We hear of a silent generation, more concerned with security than integrity, with conforming than performing, with imitating than creating.
> —THOMAS J. WATSON

THE PETER PIONEER

The early pioneers from Europe who established homesteads in America were seeking a new life in a new land. The great land grab is over, so the modern pioneer must seek his new life in a land that has already been discovered. Today, we need the pioneering spirit more urgently than ever. Pioneering requires acute awareness of what is going on, in contrast to the heedless inattentiveness of many of today's rut-bound settlers. The pioneer starts by expanding his or her consciousness so as to think of things as they might be and then uses creative imagination by adding some desirable qualities or subtracting some inferior or needless elements. A pioneer may be either the first person or a member of the first group to explore a new area.

> As life is action and passion, it is required of man
> that he should share the passion and action of his
> time, at peril of being judged not to have lived.
> —OLIVER WENDELL HOLMES

GEORGE (CRUSADER IN THE SWAMPS) MATTHEWS * Matthews hardly gives the impression of a crusader. He is a pensioner of modest means, who leans on a cane as he limps along his beloved shoreline of southwest Florida. Much of this area still consists of mangrove swamps, but developers are moving into the area, filling the wetlands, building high-rise hotels and condominiums.

Matthews hardly gives the impression of a crusader.

* Author's Note: We have returned to the present to examine conversion strategies by which the Peter Planet may be achieved, so we are abandoning the use of fictitious names for the balance of the book.

As a child, George C. Matthews explored these swamps while on fishing trips and resolved then to preserve them so that children in the years to come could have an opportunity to engage in the same wholesome activities.

A boy's will is the wind's will,
And the thoughts of youth are long, long thoughts.
—H. W. LONGFELLOW

In addition to his sentiments, Matthews has the scientific evidence with which to refute the exploiters and developers. Not only are the swamps the habitat of wildlife and a spawning ground for many of the commercial fish in the Gulf of Mexico, but the mangrove roots prevent erosion of the coastline.

The happiest man is he who learns from nature the lesson of worship.
—R. W. EMERSON

What makes it possible for Matthews to be a formidable obstacle to the land destroyers is that he has been a law student. Although he never practiced law he has become an expert on land regulations. His investigations show that most of the coastal swamp is tidal land and therefore belongs to the people of Florida or the federal government. Many of his victorious legal battles, resolved before reaching the public expense of the trial stage, were based on various laws that forbid dredging and filling operations in tidal lands. Other victories were based on the legal grounds that the United States owns the unsurveyed islands lying offshore.

In 1971, Matthews conducted a unique battle away from his home territory. On hearing of the plans to augment the already adequate security precautions surrounding ex-President Nixon's Biscayne Bay house by dredging and filling in 2,000 cubic yards of tidal waters, he threatened suit. Others joined him in opposition, and the White House reluctantly abandoned the project. Although his opponents denounce his methods (presumably because they are effective), he has won many victories. He credits his amazing record of success to his strategy: "Sue the bums!"

> It is a blessed thing that in every age someone has
> had the individuality enough and courage enough
> to stand by his own convictions.
> —ROBERT G. INGERSOLL

PETERSEN, FERRAR, AND ECOLO-HAUL   In 1972, Gary Petersen, who lives at the other edge of the continent in California, decided to temporarily suspend his college education in order to do something about the waste and pollution he saw accumulating. Gary's pollution solution was to form a company, Ecolo-Haul, to recycle reusable trash such as paper, glass, and metal. He set up collection centers where people could bring their old newspapers, boxes, bags, bottles, and cans. He soon discovered that private enterprise for public good could produce a modest financial return. Lured by the prospects of also living in conspicuous poverty, his friend Bill Ferrar joined Gary in Ecolo-Haul.

Like many pioneering efforts, Gary and Bill's requires hard work, long hours, and intimate contact with heat, grime, dust, and mud. Both young men feel enriched by their enterprise, and they intend to make a career of it. They say, "We're going to stay in this business in spite of inflation and declining profits on our labor." Gary and Bill know that the higher the mountains of trash they can collect at their centers, fewer forests will be denuded and less ore and minerals stripped from the earth.

> You can't make it. You can't buy it. And when it's
> gone, it's gone forever.
> —CHIEF BUFFALO TIGER

Gary and Bill have been able to enlist the concern and active support of Los Angeles Mayor Tom Bradley, as well

*Gary and Bill turn their concern for the environment into a
livelihood.*

as civic and ecology organizations. They have been working
with the mayor's office on a plan to employ underprivileged
and handicapped workers at the collection and recycling centers. Gary says, "It's work they can do, and we feel like we're
all benefiting from it." Recently the two enthusiastic entrepre-
neurs have even hired out their services to help others on the
selection of locations and the setting up of recycling centers.

> It is because of the devotion or sacrifice of indi-
> viduals that causes become of value.
> —JULIAN HUXLEY

THE FOX   As far back as 1969, a mysterious person calling
himself "The Fox" has sneaked around fighting ecological
wrongs. He was able to maintain his anonymity even while testifying by telephone to a federal environmental committee.
This enterprising mystery man of Kane County, Illinois, took

his pseudonym from the Fox River that he vowed to protect from ever-encroaching pollution. He began his campaign against local polluters by capping, in the dead of night, spewing industrial chimneys and plugging sewage outlets of illegal polluters.

The Fox capped the chimneys and plugged the sewage outlets of illegal polluters.

"The Fox" became a pollution fighter because nothing was being done to actually stop certain industries from poisoning the air and water. He is well-aware that his tactics are not a solution, but feels that he has to wake people up. He said, "I definitely don't feel it is any more immoral for me to plug up a sewer that spills out filth than to stop a man from beating a dog or strangling a woman. I want to make it perfectly clear that I do not destroy. I just stop illegal and immoral actions."

> Liberty too can corrupt, and absolute liberty can corrupt absolutely.
> —GERTRUDE HIMMELFARB

There are countless opportunities for each of us to become involved in progressive pioneering enterprises. Your local library and bookstore can provide you with books on how to practice conservation in the home. Subjects covered include everything from planting marigolds in your garden to repel destructive insects, to lists of everyday details such as the use of white paper products, free from non-biodegradable dyes; instructions for creating useful and decorative items from materials formerly thrown away; and walking or riding a bicycle in lieu of driving, thus creating the ultimate in gasoline saving and pollution reduction.

> Every man who knows how to read has it in his power to magnify himself, to multiply the ways in which he exists, to make his life full, significant, and interesting.
> —ALDOUS HUXLEY

As a parent you can pioneer a better way of raising your children. Help them develop a sensitivity to, and an appreciation of, nature. Teach them cooperation and tolerance rather than distrust, and prepare them for the kind of world essential to human survival.

> The hand that rules the cradle rocks the world.
> —PETER DE VRIES

Through our personal commitments to conservation, through our wisdom in using our purchasing power, and through our pioneering efforts to start to improve the environment, we can change direction from a destroying, exploiting, consuming society to a using, recycling, conserving society.

> 'Tis not too late to seek a newer world.
> —ALFRED, LORD TENNYSON

CHAPTER XI

Performance

Plans to protect air and water, wilderness and
wildlife are in fact plans to protect man.
—STEWART UDALL

THE PETER PATRON

HUNDREDS of organizations, each in their own way, are already providing conversion strategies. The following consists of some descriptions of the areas of concern and partial lists of organizations worthy of your patronage.

CONSERVATION From the beginning, man imposed his will on nature. He had to in order to survive. He lacked physical strength, fangs, claws, horns, shells, and enough hair to keep him warm, but he was superior to all other creatures in his adaptive behavior. He made tools and weapons and clothed himself in the skins of other animals. He set fire to the forest to drive out the game. He ate the birds and beasts and planted seeds in the cleared land. If the land eroded he moved on. He domesticated cattle, sheep, and goats that grazed the grassland down to its roots and left a desert. He moved on to greener fields and nature either healed the wounds, if they were minor, or if they were major, the land lay barren for eons while the desert slowly developed its own ecology.

186

Earth felt the wound, and
Nature from her seat
Sighing through all her works gave
signs of woe,
That all was lost.
—JOHN MILTON

Man had no inborn sense of conservation, only a sense of survival, so he adapted his behavior and his environment to that cause. The individual, tribe, or race that failed to perform the feat of adaptation became extinct.

The unfit die—the fit both live and thrive.
Alas, who says so? They who do survive.
—SARAH N. CLEGHORN

For millions of years the human population was so small that there was always plenty of new land, but in recent times the population exploded and the industrial revolution arrived, so that man had the numbers and technology to do more damage. He assaulted the land with explosives, bulldozers, chemical fertilizers, pesticides, defolients, and weed killers. He slaughtered the animals, poisoned the earth, and destroyed their habitat. In bending nature to his will, man has come perilously close to destroying his own life-support system.

The sun, the moon and the stars would have disappeared long ago . . . had they happened to be
within reach of predatory human hands.
—HAVELOCK ELLIS

It is too late to turn back. We have altered too much to let nature take its course. Our survival now depends on accepting responsibility for our planet's well-being. This is the survival skill for our age. We must learn how to convert our global environment into a permanent place to live. It will take time and intelligence and effort to learn how to create man-made ecological systems that are compatible with natural cycles, but we have the technology and brain power to do it.

In every age there is a turning point, a new way of
seeing and asserting the coherence of the world.
—J. BRONOWSKI

Although nature provides the rules, and the examples of
how ecological cycles operate, man-made ecological systems
are not a product of back-to-nature sentimentality. Nature is
everything beautiful that our earth provides, but nature is also
tornadoes, earthquakes, volcanoes, floods, freezing cold, torrid
heat, fleas, lice, mosquitoes, termites, scorpions, tapeworms,
tuberculosis, cancer, syphilis, malaria, and rats. The purpose
of man-made ecological systems is to protect man's life-support system and some of the beauty of nature. To achieve this
requires protection of selected areas of the planet in a wilderness state and protection of a great variety of flora and fauna.
As a conversion strategy we must conserve as much as possible
so that an environment exists for the transition to permanent
man-made ecological systems.

Environmental preservation calls for a redirection
of our technological efforts, as well as a restructuring of patterns of consumption.
—NEIL H. JACOBY

The conservation field offers you the opportunity to become
a member of a society as specialized as Ducks Unlimited or
as general as the International Union for the Conservation of
Nature and National Resources.

Ducks, Unlimited. P.O. Box 66300, Chicago, Ill. 60666.
This organization works to conserve wild waterfowl in the
United States and Canada.

Environmental Defense Fund, Inc. 162 Old Town Road,
East Setauket, N.Y. 11733.
This fund is used, with outstanding success, for environmental
defense in court cases.

Friends of the Earth. 30 East 42 St., New York, N.Y. 10017.

This aggressive, international conservation organization works for legislation to protect the environment.

International Union for the Conservation of Nature and Natural Resources. 1110 Morges, Geneva, Switzerland.
This union of conservation groups provides information on everything from conservation to instructions on gardening.

National Audubon Society. 1130 Fifth Ave., New York, N.Y. 10038.
This is a vigorous group in all aspects of conservation.

Sierra Club. 1050 Mills Tower, San Francisco, Calif. 94104.
This club has an outstanding record as a fighter in the defense of our natural resources.

World Wildlife Fund. 910 Seventeenth St., N.W., Washington, D.C. 20006.
This fund is devoted to insuring a living wildlife heritage for this planet.

> This could be such a beautiful world
> if we could all care just a little more.
> —ROSALIND WELCHER

PROTECTION OF CONSUMERS AND CITIZENS   There are literally thousands of anti-social lobbies and special interest groups. In contrast, there are only a few organizations that are independent, nonpartisan, and devoted to protection of the citizen and consumer. Here are some of the highly successful ones working in your interest.

Common Cause. Box 220, Washington, D.C. 20044.
This organization, founded in 1970 by John Gardner, has become a truly effective citizens' lobby.

Consumers Education and Protective Association. 6048 Ogontoy Ave., Philadelphia, Pa. 19141.

This association provides distribution of consumer protection information.

League of Women Voters Education Fund. 1730 M St., N.W., Washington, D.C. 20036.
This organization of concerned women studies public issues and publishes well-reasoned statements.

Public Citizen, Inc. P.O. Box 19404, Washington, D.C. 20036.
This is a public-action citizen group initiated by Ralph Nader that is involved in many areas of citizen protection.

> Make the system correct itself.
> —E. CONTINI

PEACE   The ultimate objectives of these organizations are to improve international relations, prevent wars, and make international law effective.

United Nations Association of the United States of America. 833 UN Plaza, New York, N.Y. 10017.
This is a private, nonpartisan association of people who want to prevent war through strengthening the United Nations as a force for reason and peaceful progress for the whole world.

World Federalists, USA. 2029 K St., N.W., Washington, D.C. 20006.
The motto of this organization is "World peace through world law." This becomes increasingly relevant with the growing realization that many problems are global and that solutions must transcend the limits of national borders.

The Fund for Peace. 1855 Broadway, New York, N.Y. 10023.
This fund supports a wide range of educational and research activities, including international studies. A unique and valuable service is performed by its Center for Defense Information in Washington, D.C. Under the direction of Rear Admiral

Gene R. La Rocque, USN (Ret.), it scrutinizes defense policies and budgets and publishes its findings in the *Defense Monitor*.

> Peace is better than war, because in peace the sons
> bury their fathers, but in war the fathers bury their
> sons.
>
> —CROESUS

POPULATION   Actualization of the Peter Planet depends upon integrated progress in conservation, protection of consumers and citizens, and peace. But all of these efforts will end in failure if the problem of overpopulation is not resolved and we live for today with no thought for the morrow.

> We all worry about the population explosion—but
> we don't worry about it at the right time.
>
> —A. HOPPE

The facts are that at the time of the fall of Rome there were about 400 million people on planet earth. By 1600 there were 1 billion; by 1900 there were 2 billion; by 1960 there were 3 billion; and by the year 2000 there may be 6 billion. In spite of increased food supplies, half the people in the world today are hungry and millions are near the point of starvation. But the idea that food is the most important issue is a dangerous misconception of the population problem. It implies that the main point of human endeavor from now on should be to see how many persons can be kept alive on the surface of this planet. This is a meaningless or empty view of the purpose of human life. Success in multiplying production of food in an effort to keep up with population would culminate in even greater suffering when the limited resources of our planet became insufficient to feed further increases in the numbers of people.

There appears to be irrefutable evidence that the

mere fact of physical overcrowding induces violence.

—HARVEY WHEELER

An American child uses twenty-five to fifty times as much
of the earth's resources as an African or Indian child. It is
part of our American mythology that we can help the backward countries by bringing them up to *Our Way of Life*. The
absurdity in this myth is the fact that the American Way of
Life depends on the underdeveloped countries' supplying us
with *their* resources.

Every absurdity has a champion to defend it.

—OLIVER GOLDSMITH

Reproduction should be more than just having children. It
should include raising them to have a decent life. Parents, the
world over, should be encouraged to have one or two well-
cared-for children. The following organizations are working
toward that goal.

Planned Parenthood Federation of America, Inc. 810 Seventh
Ave., New York, N.Y. 10019.
This effective agency was founded by Margaret Sanger and
is a member of the International Planned Parenthood Federation. It provides information and direct service through birth
control clinics.

Zero Population Growth. 367 State St., Los Altos, Calif.
94022.
This is a grass-roots population control movement with the
specific objective of achieving a condition of no population
increase.

Negative Population Growth, Inc. 103 Park Ave., New York,
N.Y. 10007.
This is a new organization with a specific objective to achieve
fewer people for a better world.

> Our planet could feed many more people than it
> can support in dignity and freedom. The spatial
> requirements for a mentally healthy life are much
> larger than the requirements set by food produc-
> tion.
>
> —KONRAD LORENZ

THE PETER PEN

The *written word* has long been a mightier influence in
changing man's ideas and behavior than the spoken promise.
Rachel Carson's *Silent Spring* warned about the dangers of
DDT and other chemical pesticides and started a wave of
protest that eventually resulted in official action to limit the
use of these poisons. Paul Ehrlich's *The Population Bomb*
presented frightening, fact-based forecasts that impressed read-
ers with the need for increased support of population control
measures. Ralph Nader's *Unsafe at Any Speed* created a new
awareness of the need for improved automobile safety.

> I think the whole glory of writing lies in the fact
> that it forces us out of ourselves into the lives of
> others.
>
> —SHERWOOD ANDERSON

Books and articles are invaluable in communicating an
overall plan or in presenting an adequate explanation of a
complex solution. If you lack the time to do the research and
writing required for books and articles, you can still be an
effective author who promotes positive conversion strategies.

> Research is to see what everybody else has seen,
> and to think what nobody else has thought.
>
> —ALBERT SZENT-GYORGYI

If every day each Senator and Representative received intelligent letters demanding responsible action on specific problems, there would be substantial improvement in our politics.

To be the most effective, letters should be short and precise requesting specific action. The most effective letter is one page that expresses your concern and then asks for information or makes a recommendation about one topic.

> A word to the wise is not enough, if it doesn't make any sense.
>
> —JAMES THURBER

Write letters of complaint that demand responsible action to managers of companies that pollute or make shoddy merchandise, overpackaged goods, and throwaway products. But also write encouraging letters praising those who say and do the responsible thing. Your approval, clearly expressed in a letter to the individual or to the editor of your newspaper, makes the politician, company manager, or shopkeeper more confident that he or she is on the right track.

> Words are one of our chief means of adjusting to all situations of life. The better control we have over words, the more successful our adjustment is likely to be.
>
> —BERGEN EVANS

THE PETER PROTAGONIST

The Peter Protagonist is one who plays a vital role in solving problems and who continues to inspire others to participate. He or she is similar to a Peter Pioneer, but the Protagonist is more involved in an active leadership role.

> It is hard to look up to a leader who keeps his ear to the ground.
>
> —JAMES H. BOREN

ANDREW LIPKIS   The prediction was that the San Bernardino National Forest, one of California's most beautiful recreational areas, would be a desert within twenty-five years. Smog was killing the Jeffrey and ponderosa pines. To avert this prediction, sixteen-year-old Andrew Lipkis set out to replant the forest with smog-resistant trees.

For Andrew, planting trees was more than just digging in the dirt.

It was during the summers that Andrew, who grew up in Los Angeles, had been able to escape to the mountains. In 1970 he began a serious study of the problem of dying trees. He learned how smog destroyed the chlorophyll in the needles and how this reduced photosynthesis, so that the trees could not utilize the water and minerals essential to life. Saddened by the browning of the evergreens, and knowing that Sierra redwood, incense cedar, and sugar pine could survive the smog, Andrew conceived a plan.

In 1970, he put his ideas to the test by approaching some of the businesses engaged in advertising themselves as "ecological companies." During one visit he talked with a public relations official who told him, "I was just up in the forest and it looked fine to me." This and similar encounters with

vested interests opened the eyes of the sixteen-year-old re-
former to the PR mentality. "It wasn't a total loss," he re-
marked, "I developed a real awareness of people who were
trying to con me."

In 1971, his senior year at University High School, Andrew
became involved in a student film project and made a movie
about the dying trees, which was shown on a local educational
television station.

In 1972, Andrew wrote to the Datsun Company regarding
their Plant-A-Tree advertising campaign, proposing that they
support his tree-planting project. During the usual corporate
foot-dragging, the State Department ruled coincidentally that
no foreign company could engage in this country's domestic
affairs. The Datsun program had to be cancelled and Andrew
learned another lesson about both corporate structure and
government: bureaucratic deadwood won't grow trees.

In 1973, Andrew discovered that the California State Division of Forestry possessed 20,000 sugar pine seedlings. The
division grows seedlings but does not have a budget to plant
them. If they were not sold by April, they would have to be
destroyed. When Andrew asked if he could have the seedlings
that they could not sell, he was told that regulations didn't
allow the giving away of state property. If he could not produce $600 by the April deadline, the 20,000 trees would be
plowed under. Lipkis called the nursery regularly. One day
they told him that 12,000 of the seedlings had just been destroyed. When the problem was detailed to Art Seidenbaum,
a columnist for the *Los Angeles Times,* phone calls were
made to Sacramento, embarrassing questions were asked, and
a revealing newspaper story was promised. Eight thousand
trees were immediately presented to Andrew—free.

The events that followed demonstrated Andrew's organiza-
tional and leadership ability as well as the generosity of many
individuals who wanted to help. While continuing his college
classes, majoring in environmental studies, Andrew managed

to keep his seedlings dormant, until he could transplant them, by storing them in donated space in commercial and domestic refrigerators. Then he obtained 8,000 milk cartons from a dairy and a container company. His college friends and a local Boy Scout troop helped pot the individual seedlings in the milk cartons. The little trees were watered and kept shaded until college recessed for the summer. Businesses donated transportation and tools for planting. Andrew, along with volunteer foresters, worked with groups of campers to dig holes, gently set the seedlings, and keep them watered for the remainder of the summer. Andrew, nineteen, had cut through the entanglement of red tape, had overcome bureaucratic nonresponsiveness, and had planted 8,000 smog-resistant trees.

In 1974 and 1975, Andrew Lipkis again took to the San Bernardino mountains, where he continued to plant trees and put down roots for future generations.

> At nineteen, everything is possible and tomorrow looks friendly.
>
> —JIM BISHOP

RALPH NADER   Ralph Nader's fame began in 1964 when his book on automobile safety, *Unsafe at Any Speed,* was published. In the years since then Nader's crusades have expanded to include pollution, pesticides, exploitation of the Amercian Indian, unsanitary conditions in the fish and meat industries, radiation hazards from X-rays used by doctors and dentists, unsafe pipelines, and many other consumer issues.

Nader's parents brought him up to possess the passionate idealism and determination that have inspired his "Nader's Raiders" and other coworkers to pursue the truth arduously and relentlessly. When he says, "I place the needs of our society above my own ambitions," he is convincing in both word and deed. He works eighteen to twenty hours a day, seven days a week. He does not own a television set or automobile and lives in a ninety-dollar-a-month apartment in Washington,

Although his personal life is modest, his public achievements
are impressive.

D.C. Although his personal life is modest, his public achievements are impressive. He was influential in stopping the manufacture of the accident-prone Corvair by General Motors and in the passing of legislation such as the Radiation Control for Health and Safety Act, Wholesome Meat Act, National Gas Pipeline Safety Act, and other consumer-oriented acts. Nader has acquired a level of credibility rare in these times. One reason for this is that he researches his information so thoroughly that he is rarely wrong. Congressmen, citizens, and businessmen pay attention to the hazards he exposes and frequently take action to protect the consumer. Nader has made consumerism a popular movement.

> You don't set a fox to watching the chickens just because he has a lot of experience in the hen house.
>
> —HARRY S. TRUMAN

"Doc" Loutzenhiser   When Dr. Donald Loutzenhiser resolves to do something, he goes all the way. He decided to
help clean up the city of San Bernardino by picking up recyclable trash every Saturday, but in making his rounds he
hit upon a scheme to avoid polluting the air. The vehicle used
to gather the piles of newspapers, aluminum, glass, and steel
items collected by volunteers is a no exhaust-emitting truck.
When "Doc" says he operates on four horsepower he is literally
correct. He is referring to an ancient dray hitched to four
magnificent Belgian roans.

When "Doc" decides to do something, he goes all the way.

Although he hasn't made any money on his "Saturday job"
or, in fact, broken even, this has not put a damper on his
spirit. Loutzenhiser believes that there is a serious need both
for recycling trash and for using horses instead of motor
vehicles. Opponents to his ideas generally charge that horses
will pollute the streets in a different manner. Doc has solved
this problem, however. When he makes his Saturday rounds

he carries a scoop shovel and bucket. With that objection met, he sees no reason not to expand to four wagons and sixteen horses. He may not be making a profit with this business, but Doc Loutzenhiser is certainly "cleaning up."

> If all the perverted ingenuity which was put into making automobiles had only gone into improving the breed of horses, we might be a lot better off today.
>
> —JOE GOULD

PAUL SOGLIN   In April 1973, twenty-seven-year-old Paul Soglin became Mayor of Madison, Wisconsin, by defeating the conservative incumbent, Mayor Dyke. Soglin, while a student at the University of Wisconsin, had been an activist in the antiwar movement. After graduate school he ran for city council in Madison's Eighth District, in which students comprised a majority of the voters. As an alderman he learned about municipal government and studied problems such as transportation, housing, zoning, and sewer maintenance.

In 1973, Soglin entered the race for mayor as an independent and won with 52 percent of the vote. His student supporters may have been disappointed when, at his inaugural celebration, he took off his dress shirt to reveal a T-shirt bearing the legend MELLOW MAN. Mayor-elect Soglin said, "It's going to take mellow men and mellow women to put this city together in the next two years."

During his first term of office, he made substantial progress and, despite an occasional leaning toward levity, was re-elected in 1975. By focusing on the city's problems and working persistently toward their solution, he has attracted considerable support. The more radical of his backers are critical of his slowness in bringing about changes, and the more conservative element among the merchants that formerly controlled the city are critical of his too-rapid changes. Somewhere between

Paul (Mellow Man) Soglin had a new sign made for his office door.

these extremes Soglin derives enough support so that he can be effective.

Improvements in public transportation have resulted in a 17 percent increase in the number of riders. He has involved more women and members of minority groups in civic government. He has tightened housing inspection procedures and started a fund to supply loans for home rehabilitation. Although these may not appear to be spectacular achievements, they demonstrate that a Peter Protagonist in politics can receive substantial citizen support through focusing on problems and solutions, rather than on the needs of self-serving political groups.

> The liberal is accustomed to appearing radical
> to conservatives, counterrevolutionary to radicals,
> and as a fink to activists of all persuasions.
> —HARRY S. ASHMORE

DENIS MARSHALL   Due to the fighting spirit shown by Denis Marshall and through the accumulated strength of many individual efforts, the people of Salmon Arm, a beautifully unspoiled village in British Columbia, have fought their battle against the throwaway soft drink container and won. When the bottle companies in the area decided to switch to non-returnable containers, Denis Marshall, publisher of the *Salmon Arm Observer,* faced up to the challenge. He published a continuous barrage of editorials, cartoons, and feature stories that aroused the community's fighting spirit. Town meetings were held, and many people in the village became personally involved. Joe Buresh, Salmon Arm bowling alley operator, found a simple but very effective way to help. He took a financial risk by refusing the one-way bottles sent to him by his soft drink supplier and switched to a brand using deposit bottles. Diana Dombroski, wife of a local schoolteacher, shared Marshall's indignation and convinced the local government to support the crusade. The determination of Denis Marshall spread. Supermarket managers were forced by customer pressure to carry returnables again. Citizens joined the Bottle Boycott, as they realized that the result of apathy and inaction would be a litterbug community.

The effective Salmon Arm Bottle Boycott appeared to be the catalyst for far-reaching changes. Today, by law, all nonreturnable beer and soft drink bottles, as well as cans, are illegal in the entire province of British Columbia.

He makes righteousness readable.
—JAMES BONE

JOHN GARDNER   "America is not the nation it set out to be," says John W. Gardner. As founder and chairman of Common Cause, he is the leader of the only national citizens' lobby devoted to the reform, renewal, and restoration required to put the country back on the road to responsive and responsible government. After spending five years in Washington as Secre-

Citizens joined Denis Marshall in the Bottle Boycott

tary of Health, Education and Welfare and as Chairman of the Urban Coalition, Gardner was convinced that only an aroused and organized citizenry could revitalize government and change the nation's disastrous course. He said, "When people are serving, life is no longer meaningless."

Common Cause is a lobby of a different type from those of private enterprise because it represents all citizens' interests. It is an antidote for the present system that collects revenue from the unorganized taxpayer and distributes it to powerfully organized industrial and special interest groups. Gardner founded Common Cause because he believes that we have allowed the political process to decay through lack of active participation, but that it is not too late to revitalize the system. Common Cause has conducted investigations into military spending, environmental problems, the congressional seniority system, conflicts of interest, campaign spending, and many other governmental areas. Gardner says, "When one pays out

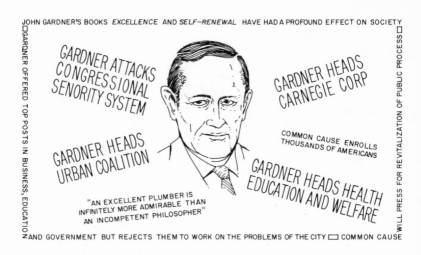

JOHN GARDNER'S BOOKS *EXCELLENCE* AND *SELF-RENEWAL* HAVE HAD A PROFOUND EFFECT ON SOCIETY □

□GARDNER OFFERED TOP POSTS IN BUSINESS, EDUCATION

GARDNER ATTACKS CONGRESSIONAL SENORITY SYSTEM

GARDNER HEADS CARNEGIE CORP

GARDNER HEADS URBAN COALITION

COMMON CAUSE ENROLLS THOUSANDS OF AMERICANS

"AN EXCELLENT PLUMBER IS INFINITELY MORE ADMIRABLE THAN AN INCOMPETENT PHILOSOPHER"

GARDNER HEADS HEALTH EDUCATION AND WELFARE

WILL PRESS FOR REVITALIZATION OF PUBLIC PROCESS□

AND GOVERNMENT BUT REJECTS THEM TO WORK ON THE PROBLEMS OF THE CITY ☐ COMMON CAUSE

He saw his job as a series of great opportunities brilliantly disguised as insoluble problems.

over two million dollars to presidential and congressional campaigns, the U. S. government is virtually up for sale." Through Common Cause, the will of the citizen is being done. It is not a third party but a nonpartisan third force based on the concept that the things that unite us are more important than the things that divide us. Gardner said that he saw his new job as a series of great opportunities brilliantly disguised as insoluble problems. He went on to state, "The cynic says, 'One man can't do anything.' I say, "Only one man can do anything." John Gardner is living proof of what one man can do.

> You'll find in no park or city
> A monument to a committee.
> —VICTORIA PASTERNACK

CHAPTER XII

Prospect

We must stop talking about the American dream
and start listening to the dreams of Americans.
—GOVERNOR REUBIN ASKEW

ULTIMATELY the Peter Plan must involve the political process. The prospect of a viable future depends on changes
within the political system.

I have been told I was on the road to hell, but I
had no idea it was just a mile down the road with
a dome on it.
—ABRAHAM LINCOLN

THE PETER POLL

It is usually possible for a political candidate to be elected
on a basis of rather vague promises. The voters are frequently
disappointed to discover that the campaign oratory had little
to do with their man's intentions. The reasons for this apparent
duplicity is that financial investors in the campaign usually
have more control over the politician than do the needs of
the country.

I always voted at my party's call,
And I never thought of thinking for myself at all.
—WILLIAM S. GILBERT

205

A second reason for disappointment in the political process as a means of long-range problem solving has been the lack of a comprehensive and specific enough plan as a campaign platform. The voter is seldom presented with a plan of sufficient scope to capture his vision of a better world. Instead he is presented with a series of thirty-second commercials in which the candidate makes extravagant declarations about his patriotism and unique capability to solve all problems, while covertly or overtly assassinating the character of his opponent. When elected, the politician may surprise all concerned by acting (1) wisely, (2) foolishly, or (3) corruptly.

> The short memories of American voters is what keeps our politicians in office.
>
> —WILL ROGERS

The politician who says whatever is expedient or who plays the fool, captures the attention of the media. The corrupt politician seldom shows up as corrupt until after great harm has been done to the political process. The wise and honest politician can protect the integrity of the process, and may have the charisma to get elected, but still lack a comprehensive plan for solving the problems that put us in jeopardy.

It is better to elect a wise and honest politician than it is to elect a crooked or weak one. But, if you are concerned about the future, you had better find and elect a wise and honest individual who has a comprehensive plan for solving our complex and interrelated problems. Isolated, short-term measures, no matter how well intentioned, will not divert us for long from their traumatic consequences.

> There is no worse heresy than that the office sanctifies the holder of it.
>
> —LORD ACTON

How can you identify the candidate you are looking for? Insist that each candidate for political office—local, state, or national—endorse a comprehensive and specific plan for a better world before he or she will receive your vote. Begin by writing to the candidate, explaining that he or she must identify the specifics that will be implemented if elected. Insist that he or she take a written pledge to do so and that the signed document be made public. For example, the pledge could consist of items such as: If elected—

> I will consistently support clean air, pure water and other environmental protection legislation,
> I will sponsor the Pay-As-You-Pollute Bill,
> I will initiate action to establish comprehensive development of nonpolluting, renewable energy sources, and the creation of a national electricity grid,
> I will propose substantial funding of peace research and world law as part of our national defense program.

Convince the candidate that you will not be satisfied with political expediency and pledge that you and other like-thinking persons will support efforts for long-range planning if futurists, ecologists, and experts in systems dynamics are brought into the planning process.

> The basis of our political system is the right of the people to make and to alter their constitutions of government.
> —GEORGE WASHINGTON

Communicate your dissatisfaction with the piecemeal, hodge-podge legislation that uses your tax dollars for the highway fund but not for a total transportation system. Tell your candidate that you will not have one of your tax dollars going to support the Department of Agriculture's tobacco subsidy while another goes to Health, Education and Welfare's anti-smoking campaign. Make it clear that you want commonsense, rational, responsible government.

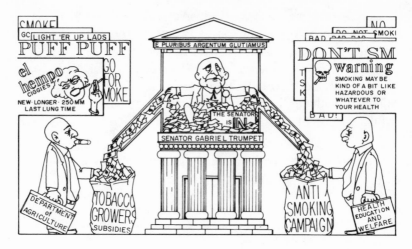

*Tell your candidate that you will not have one of your tax dollars
subsidizing tobacco while another supports the
anti-smoking campaign.*

THE PETER POLITICIAN

A great many people are pessimistic about the future. This
is understandable, as we continue to rationalize our absurdities
and proliferate our problems. Mass pessimism brings about
a self-contemptuous culture, where expressions of self-hatred
gain ready acceptance. Combined pessimism and self-con-
tempt drain the courage of the individual and leave only fear,
guilt, and a pervasive sense of unworthiness. This pessimistic
attitude is expressed by the news commentator who suggests
that all politicians are dishonest. It is expressed in the classroom where the teacher encourages criticism but is cynical
about solutions. It is expressed by the citizen who believes that
it makes no difference who is elected because, "they're all
alike." It is expressed by a hedonistic citizenry that sacrifices
the future for present, transitory pleasures.

We can destroy ourselves by cynicism and disillusion, just as effectively as by bombs.

—KENNETH CLARK

Pessimism leads to a reaction against reason, and the politician who offers naive optimism may appear to be a savior. Widespread pessimism is the environment in which a dictator flourishes. Even in a democracy, the pessimist expects little of a political leader except to be a father figure who provides comforting slogans and simplistic solutions.

For every credibility gap there is a gullibility fill.

—RICHARD CLOPTON

Pessimists fail to select leadership from among the ablest, best-educated, and most articulate, because pessimism is a two-edged sword. An attitude of contempt for the common man flourishes among some of the most educated and intelligent citizens, while these same gifted and articulate members of our society decline the responsibility of leadership. Part of the reason for this is that when an educated, articulate, intelligent citizen does offer to serve, his motives immediately become suspect by the pessimists.

Bad officials are elected by good citizens who do not vote.

—GEORGE JEAN NATHAN

A prime function of the political leader is to keep hope alive, but not by false promises and simplistic slogans. If you are one of those indomitable individuals with a persistent impulse to replace brutality with reason, inequity with justice, ignorance with enlightenment, an impulse too strong to be squelched by the current fashion of despair, you should consider whether becoming a Peter Politician may be your role.

One of the saddest experiences which can ever come to a human being is to awaken, gray-haired and wrinkled, near the close of an unproductive

career, to the fact that all through the years he
has been using only a small part of himself.

—V. W. Burrows

THE PETER PERSISTENCE

If the Peter Program, discussed so far, is implemented, one
more important ingredient is still required—*persistence*. True
progress, socially and politically, must be based on honest
communication. Without it, society becomes a battleground
of deception and a wasteland of half-truths. We must persist
in the truth and demand honesty from the representatives of
our institutions, and our politicians in particular.

Politicians make strange bedfellows, but they all
share the same bunk.

—W. I. E. Gates

To persistently influence a politician's activities you first
should have his commitments on specific measures. From
that point on, reinforce him with approving letters, telegrams,
phone calls, editorials, and letters to the editor for every gain
he makes toward that objective. A politician, like any other
member of society, is sensitive to approval. If a substantial
portion of his constituency expresses praise of his positive actions and conversion strategies toward the Peter Planet he
will want to maintain that direction.

Our country—when right, to be kept right, when
wrong, to be put right.

—Carl Schurz

So far as we presently know, we are living on the only
planet that is fit for human habitation. If this earth were unlimited in size and resources we could continue our economy
of expansion. Our survival depends on our willingness to re-
shape society to the ecological facts of life. Scientific research
can reveal the severity of the crisis we are facing, but only

persistent planned social change and persistent political action can resolve it.

> The most powerful factors in the world are clear
> ideas in the minds of energetic men of good will.
> —J. ARTHUR THOMSON

*I believed then and I still believe that this is the
only planet fit for man.*

Postscript

> We are healthy only to the extent that our ideas
> are humane.
> —KURT VONNEGUT, JR.

I RESIDE on the planet Earth, a circumstance I share with
more than three billion other human beings in this year of
1975. I am among the Earth's inhabitants who are well fed
and able to live "the good life." This means that I can take
time to think and write about the future.

I live in a deteriorating environment that threatens my
health, happiness, and survival. Billions of my fellow inhabitants merely subsist. Many are starving. Overpopulation and
overexploitation of Earth are endangering our mutual habitat.

> It is impossible to experience one's death objec-
> tively and still carry a tune.
> —WOODY ALLEN

Although the problems facing mankind today are over-
whelming, The Peter Plan does not advocate going back to
the "Good Old Days" (which were not so good for the vast
majority, but may look good to some in retrospect). The past
cannot be recaptured anyway. The only successful way out of
the present crisis is to break through to a new and more advanced civilization. Strategies aimed at putting us back where

we were will ultimately cause the crisis to deepen. Attempts to get our old industrial economy back on an even keel will fail. Our concepts of progress must be reevaluated. Escalation of the GNP and increased consumerism is no longer progress. On our overexploited and finite planet, an economy based on constant expansion—more and bigger automobiles, more highways, more product obsolescence, and more mountains of discarded affluence—will have to be abandoned.

> All economic forces operate to promote and hasten annihilation; none operate against it.
> —KENNETH E. F. WATT

Achievement of an ecologically sound economy based on renewable resources would be true progress today. Moving forward through improving the quality of life—escalating pleasure, love, knowledge, skill, and actualization of human potential for concern and creativity in the service and protection of the only planet we have—is the challenge of progress today. There is no limit to growth in that direction. If we persist with the obsolete notion of growth we will commit planetary suicide in the not too distant future.

> We are confronted with insurmountable opportunities.
> —POGO (WALT KELLY)

The Peter Plan does not attempt to describe all of the conversion strategies for the transition from a destructive economy to a society based on Good and Sensible Ways. A fully developed set of such strategies requires the participation of many individuals. Some conversion strategies will emerge from the participation of concerned individuals and some will be provided by experts in the technologies required for creating complex man-made ecological systems.

> Every animal leaves traces of what it was; man alone leaves traces of what he created.
> —J. BRONOWSKI

The Peter Plan does not include the yet unknown technological developments that will inevitably influence our future, but presents only those choices we already know we can make in light of present knowledge. Looking ahead and foretelling the future has always fascinated mankind.

> Perhaps the greatest impulse to trying to foresee and plan the future comes from the combination of having new tools with which to do it and the growing realization that every technological and social innovation has repercussions which spread like a wave through the complex interlocked sections of society.
>
> —WARD MADDEN

If we try only to develop programs for solving the problems of peace and conservation and population and power, we will miss the unifying, comprehensive nature of an enduring solution. What confronts us is not a problem of energy, population, pollution of land, air, and water. The symptoms appear in the environment but the disease is human behavior motivated by false notions of growth and progress.

> Pollution and the other environmental problems are but symptoms and the disease itself is so much more deeply imbedded in our society that attack on the symptoms alone can be but a minor palliative.
>
> —ALEXANDER KING

The evidence is clear that we have the ability to resolve our difficulties and establish a new relationship to our planet based on the principles of the enduring cycles of nature. We have eliminated or controlled the major contagious diseases that plagued mankind. We have witnessed the disappearance of the killing "pea soup" London fog. The Clean Air Act of 1956 banned the burning of soft coal. London now has twice as much winter sunshine. We have banned the use of DDT in many areas and seen the return of baby brown pelicans and observed other signs of environmental recovery. There are amongst us, futurists, conservationists, ecologists, scientists and engineers, who have the knowledge we need to make the right choice. The question is not, "Can we?" but, "Will we?"

> Science may have found a cure for most evils;
> but it has found no remedy for the worst of them
> all—the apathy of human beings.
>   —HELEN KELLER

Technology has reached a point where it is producing more kinds of things than I really want, more kinds of things than I really need, and more kinds of things than I can really live with. But present technology is an erratic rocket bound to self-destruct unless its guidance system is repaired.

> Despite the very serious nature of the threat to
> environmental preservation, the inherent inertia of
> our system will probably block effective action at
> least until public concern is galvanized by some
> catastrophic disaster.
>   —MICHAEL KITZMILLER

Each day we delay voluntary implementation of conversion strategies is a day closer to doomsday. When will you be ready to take action? Will the next disaster be the one that prompts your corrective action or will it be the point of no return? I cannot answer these questions. *The next move is up to you.*

> In the fight for survival, a tie or split decision sim-
> ply will not do.
>   —MERLE L. MEACHAM

In casting myself in the role of a futurist, I am optimistic in the face of nuclear proliferation, international tensions, global pollution, and the dull despair of so many of my contemporaries. I am optimistic because of mankind's extraordinary comprehensiveness. Every other living species is highly specialized by comparison. Only the human brain seems to be able to comprehend concepts and principles. It is this comprehensiveness that will help us in the future. Many of our problems result from our overreliance on specialization that precludes comprehensive thinking. No matter how elaborate our technology, it is superficial if it is not subjected to comprehensive thinking.

> The man we call a specialist today was formerly called a man with a one-track mind.
> —ENDRE BALOGH

The Peter Plan is not a blueprint for a Peter Paradise. A Utopia tends to be a promised land set apart from the real world. To most people, the word "Utopian" means *impossible to achieve*. The Peter Plan is a possible process or way of life, not an end to be achieved. It is not a perfect system for perfect human beings, but it requires that we develop conversion strategies based on new rules and new priorities so that progress toward a new level of civilization is accomplished with attention to the long-range effects of what we do.

> Perfection of means and confusion of ends seem to characterize our age.
> —ALBERT EINSTEIN

Index